Logistics Real Estate

To Tran Quach • Michael Trübestein
Matthias Daniel Aepli

Logistics Real Estate

The Emergence of a new Asset Class

Springer Gabler

To Tran Quach
Real Estate Business Management
Swiss Life Investment Management
Zürich, Switzerland

Michael Trübestein
University of Lucerne
HSLU – Lucerne, Switzerland

Matthias Daniel Aepli
University of Lucerne
HSLU – Lucerne, Switzerland

ISBN 978-3-658-42836-5 ISBN 978-3-658-42837-2 (eBook)
https://doi.org/10.1007/978-3-658-42837-2

Gestaltung und Satz: Manuel Gächter, Oberegg
Lektorat/Planung: Guido Notthoff
This Springer Gabler imprint is published by the registered company Springer Fachmedien Wiesbaden GmbH, part of Springer Nature.
The registered company address is: Abraham-Lincoln-Str. 46, 65189 Wiesbaden, Germany

Paper in this product is recyclable.

Management Summary

Logistics plays a vital role in the economy, supplying goods to companies and households. Given its transformative impact on industries and its enduring relevance, logistics real estate has become a targeting asset class for forward-thinking investors. This research examines the evaluation criteria for logistics real estate and explores the implementation of future trends from an investor's perspective, with a specific focus on European logistics real estate as an asset class. Eight industry experts were interviewed to understand the current state of the European logistics real estate market and predict its future development, providing readers with guidance for investments.

The emergence of the Covid-19 pandemic introduced a new wave of online consumers, leading to record transaction activity in 2021. The interviewed experts anticipate the continued strength of online sales and reverse logistics (returns) in the coming years. Additionally, the pandemic exposed vulnerabilities in global supply chains, prompting a shift back to Europe and increased inventory holding, driving European logistics.

While logistics is a labor-intensive industry, Europe is experiencing a growing shortage of skilled labor. The experts predict automation will expand due to rising inflation, labor costs, occupier demand, and technological advancements. Modern logistics facilities with specific amenities will be in higher demand. Regulatory pressure to reduce carbon emissions will impact logistics real estate, potentially leading to the use of sustainable materials like timber.

The primary locations for logistics investments in Europe are metropolitan regions, supplemented by dedicated logistics areas in Germany, France, the UK, and Benelux. These locations are considered highly desirable due to their proximity to major consumption centers, favorable regulatory environments, labor availability, infrastructure connectivity, and overall cost-value proposition. Limited space availability and resistance to construction in urban areas pose challenges. Adjusting for risks associated with the political and economic climate may exert pressure on investment returns. Nevertheless, European logistics real estate remains an attractive investment opportunity with promising returns and low correlation to other asset classes.

Acknowledgments

We would like to thank everyone that made the publication of this book possible, whether through practical or moral support.

In particular, we would like to express our gratitude to our interview partners and experts in the field of logistics real estate:

- Prof. Dr. Thomas Beyerle, Managing Director & Head of Group Research, Catella Property Valuation GmbH
- Martin Haller, Chairman of the board at Basel Gateway Nord, SBB Cargo AG
- Bodo Hollung MRICS, Shareholder & Managing Director, LIP Invest GmbH
- Thomas Karmann, Global Head of Logistics, AXA Investment Managers
- Thorbjørn Pedersen, CIO, Swiss Life Asset Managers Nordics AS
- Björn Pfeiffer, Portfolio Manager of the European Industrial & Logistics (EIL) Fund, Mayfair Capital Investment Management Ltd
- Carla Seidel FRICS, Real Estate Researcher, Swiss Life Asset Managers Deutschland GmbH
- Ingo Steves, Managing Partner, BEOS Logistics GmbH

Thank you for your time and valuable contribution.

Table of Contents

List of Tables

List of Figures

1 Introduction

1

Investment opportunities are becoming increasingly rare and institutional investors are under great pressure to generate returns on their assets. While most commercial real estate asset classes such as office, brick-and-mortar retail, or hotels have been negatively affected by the measures taken to contain the pandemic, the market for logistics investments is proving to be extremely robust and crisis-resistant. One can even say that logistics real estate is flourishing. Demand for logistics space has never been so strong and thus, logistics properties are becoming increasingly attractive to institutional investors (JLL, 2021).

A range of current and continuing trends are contributing to the expanding demand for logistics capacities in Europe. Swiss Life Asset Managers (2020a, pp. 1–3) reports that logistics demand is driven by global trends such as e-commerce and the digital transformation of manufacturing. These trends in combination with other influential trends are pushing frontiers in European logistics. Besides its increasing attractiveness, the stock of logistics and industrial properties is already huge – their share in commercial real estate in Europe is estimated at a minimum of 30%. Another reason why particular attention should be paid to the European logistics market is that deglobalization is bringing back supply and demand chains to Europe. Europe has one of the densest networks of road, rail, and inland connections in the world. However, the growth in international trade and its related freight distribution systems requires the development of logistics capabilities because deglobalization is boosting demand for faster and more resilient transportation infrastructure.

Though, despite the potential of the logistics market, one must not overlook the fact that the logistics asset class also comes with its own set of challenges and pitfalls which should be considered before investing. Similarly, the

T. T. Quach et al., *Logistics Real Estate*, https://doi.org/10.1007/978-3-658-42837-2_1

climate, environmental- and sustainability aspects, as well as their impacting factors are important elements to evaluate.

Logistics properties offer investors access to a well-diversified market across sectors, use types, and regions (Swiss Life Asset Managers, 2020a, p. 10). It is relevant for investors to understand the fundamentals, current and future dynamics, and assessment criteria of logistics real estate to invest in this market. Therefore, this research is intended to provide the reader with orientation within this highly attractive asset class in a dynamic market environment. In the next subchapter, the research aim and the specific research questions are discussed in detail.

1.1 Research Aim & Questions

This research aims to underline the key dimensions behind the potential and challenges of investments in European logistics. It particularly focuses on the dynamics which shape the European logistics market. Understanding these dynamics is important to relate how logistics properties fit into the bigger picture of the economy and environment. This research is mainly targeted at institutional investors but is also suitable for interested retail investors or those interested in this industry.

This research guides the reader through an overview of logistics real estate, the key drivers affecting the European logistics market, and the current and future dynamics to finally provide a guideline for a course of action regarding investments.

The following research aim was set:

> **Investors know the fundamentals of logistics investments, and their assessment criteria and can orientate themselves within the current and future dynamics in the European logistics market.**

Considering the research aim, the following research questions were defined:

- **RQ1: What is the current situation in the European logistics market?**
- **RQ2: What are the current megatrends that are shaping European logistics?**
- **RQ3: How does the European logistics market currently look like regarding investments?**
- **RQ4: How will logistics take on ESG?**
- **RQ5: What opportunities and challenges will drive the future of European logistics?**
- **RQ6: What are recommendations for investors in terms of targeting regions, risk/return optimization, and how to implement future trends in an investment portfolio?**

1.2 Definition & Delimitation

Logistics and industrial properties are divided into two major sectors: *logistics real estate and light industrial real estate*. Important to note is that this book focuses only on logistics. The topic of light industrial is only dealt with for delimitation. Thus, this subchapter defines and distinguishes the two from each other, and further gives definition to the terms *last link/urban logistics* and *just-in-time logistics*.

Logistics Real Estate

There is no uniform definition of the term *logistics real estate*. As a rule, logistics real estate refers to buildings that serve the entire value-added chain, providing transshipment, warehousing, and all related supplementary services (DIWG, 2021, p. 40). A logistics property – usually at least 10,000m^2 in size – therefore, fulfills the need for storage, order picking, as well as distributing goods and allows for round-the-clock operations. Location-wise, a logistics property requires good transport connections, ideally by road, rail, water, and air. Logistics properties are found in metropolitan areas but also in more remote areas with proper access to transportation routes (Swiss Life Asset Managers, 2020a, p. 1).

So generally, the following distinction to industrial properties can be made: Logistics properties are typically large-scale and comprise areas with particularly good transport connections for warehousing, distribution, and, picking in European metropolitan regions, while industrial real estate is mainly represented by mixed-use commercial properties with a typically medium-sized tenant mix (Swiss Life Asset Managers, 2020b). More on the theory of logistics real estate and the different types of buildings will follow in Chapter 2: Literature Review (see Chapter 2.1: Fundamentals of Logistics).

Light Industrial Real Estate

The typology of *light industrial real estate* is not always clearly separable from other commercial or industrial buildings. The main difference lies in the higher third-party usability. Investment-intensive medium-heavy to heavy industries (e.g., mechanical engineering, turbine construction, mining, and steel production) require properties that are designed for very specific production processes and thus have low third-party usability. In contrast, light industrial properties are suitable for light forms of labor- and knowledge-intensive manufacturing of small and medium-sized consumer and investment goods. Types of uses include manufacturing, storage, office, research, and service spaces. Light industrial real estate can be more flexibly adapted to production and market cycles. As a result, light industrial real estate can be used by a broader range of parties without major conversion costs and therefore, offers great liquidity to investors (CBRE, 2021, p. 10).

The light industrial real estate sector is considered a niche sector with a very high proportion of owner-occupiers (approximately 90% in Germany). These properties often are in attractive locations within large economic areas. Different than with the logistics properties, light industrial properties are typically multi-tenanted – especially in business parks. This sector has proven high resilience in times of crisis due to the broad tenant base, especially among small and medium-sized enterprises which usually are quite loyal to their location base. Furthermore, the light industrial sector has an advantage in terms of the construction law due to the broader utilization options. On the other hand, the disadvantage of this broad use is the high asset management cost (Gütle, 2021, p. 6).

So, light industrial is the general term for mixed-used commercial property that is in or near metropolitan areas with good transport connections. These properties typically have a medium-sized multi-tenant structure although they can also include large single company occupiers. These properties can be classified into four categories (Swiss Life Asset Managers, 2020a, pp. 1–2):

- **Warehouse**: Warehouse properties offer simple storage facilities up to 10,000m^2. The size distinguishes it from logistics properties (which are at least 10,000m^2 in size).
- **Business parks**: Business parks are centrally managed and composed either of a group of separate buildings or connected rental units. They can be of all sizes and commonly provide a 20–50% office share. Typical tenants are companies involved in the light manufacturing and warehousing/logistics sector.
- **Light manufacturing**: Light manufacturing assets comprise individual objects which are utilized for diverse manufacturing purposes as well as alternative uses like storage, research, service, wholesale, and retail trading. They possess a flexible and reversible utilization structure.
- **Conversion**: Conversion properties are usually transformed and revitalized former production plants or industrial areas with potential for further densification.

Last Link / Urban Logistics

Last mile, last kilometer, and urban logistics all refer to the last link in the supply chain. Cushman & Wakefield (2019) has developed the term *last link* to refer to the final connection. The term is used regardless of whether the final connection is long or short, the delivery is by truck or electric bike, urban or rural, to a pickup location or home. For this paper, the term, and the definition according to Cushman & Wakefield will be used. In the context of e-commerce, *link* in *last link* refers to the connection to the rest of the supply chain, while *last* refers to the end of the supply chain that is reached when the package is delivered. The general rule of thumb for last link facilities is that they should be within a 30-minute drive time of major city centers and as close as possible to the first delivery point (Cushman & Wakefield, 2019).

Just-In-Time Logistics

In logistics, a delivery is referred to as *just-in-time* if a good is delivered to the customer immediately before or at the moment of need. The idea behind just-in-time logistics is to ensure that the item arrives at the warehouse at the moment the manufacturer can ship it to the customer. Thus, just-in-time logistics aims to make the supply chain leaner, minimize inventory (costs), reduce delivery time, and eliminate waste, such as unneeded items (Vector, 2021).

1.3 Methodology

This subchapter explains the methodology applied for this research paper. Before diving into the details of the research process, the composition of this paper is presented for a better understanding of the methodology.

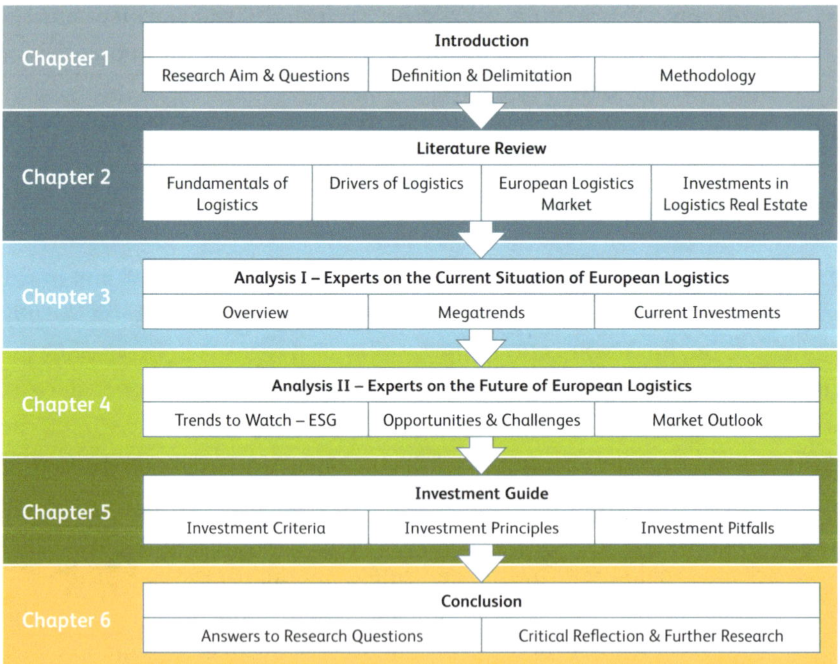

Figure 1: **Structure of the Book**

This book is composed of a total of six chapters. Chapter 1: Introduction, where the research topic is launched, the research aim and questions are defined, the definition of terms is given, as well as the applied research method is explained. Chapter 2: Literature Review, which captures existing literature in the field of European logistics real estate. The analyses are captured in chapters 3 to 5. Chapter 3: Analysis I – Experts on the Current Situation of European logistics; Chapter 4: Analysis II – Experts on the Future of European Logistics; and Chapter 5: Investment Guide. Finally, the research closes with Chapter 6: Conclusion, where the research questions are answered, the results of this work are critically reflected and a recommendation for further research is given. Figure 1 gives an overview of this book.

Research Strategy & Design

The following sections explain the applied research method in detail. First, the research strategy and design are presented.

The main six steps of a qualitative research process are applied to this research (Bell, Bryman, & Harley, 2019, pp. 357–358). Steps 1 and 2 together form the research design. In step 1, the topic *European Logistics* and the research aim are defined. In step 2, the relevant sub-topics are selected, and the corresponding research questions are specified (see Table 1: Qualitative Research Design).

To achieve the research aim set and to answer the defined research questions, steps 3 to 6 of the qualitative research process are carried out. In step 3, the data to answer the research questions are collected with a cross-sectional approach, which means the collection of data in the form of observations, on a series of variables, at a single point in time (Bell, Bryman, & Harley, 2018, pp. 58–61). For this research, academic online research in combination with semi-structured interviews is conducted. Academic online research includes the collection of existing literature about the defined topic. In the interviews, experts from this field, namely institutional investors, fund providers, and operators are surveyed using a semi-structured interview guide. Semi-structured interviews are suited to discover subjective views, orientations, and behavior related to a specific topic (Flick, 2018, p. 32). Therefore, they are appropriate to explore expert opinions on logistics investments in Europe.

Steps 4 and 5 together form the data analysis. In step 4, the results of the conducted interviews are analyzed and interpreted. In step 5, the conceptual and theoretical work is done using the data from the online research and the results of the interviews. This means relationships (similarities and differences) are investigated to reflect patterns (Bell, Bryman, & Harley, 2018, pp. 58–61). The analysis deals with the current situation of European logistics (Chapter 3: Analysis I – Experts on the Current Situation of European Logistics) and the future of European logistics (Chapter 4: Analysis II – Experts on the Future of European Logistics).

Figure 2: **Research Strategy** (Bell, Bryman, & Harley, 2019, pp. 357–358)

Step 6 deals with the findings and gives guidelines to investors (Chapter 5: Investment Guide) as well as a conclusion (Chapter 6: Conclusion). Moreover, the work is critically evaluated and the need for further research is defined. Figure 2 shows an overview of the research strategy and table 1 gives an overview of the research design (Step 1 and 2). The upcoming sections then explain the research process regarding the interviews with the experts in detail.

Table 1: **Qualitative Research Design**

What?	Why?
• Topic: Logistics Real Estate – The Emergence of a new Asset Class • Research aim: Investors know the fundamentals of logistics investments, and their assessment criteria and can orientate themselves within the current and future dynamics in the European logistics market. • Answering the research questions defined in Chapter 1.1: Research Aim & Questions.	• Investment opportunities become increasingly rare. Investors are under pressure to generate returns on their assets. • Logistics properties are becoming increasingly attractive to institutional investors. • It is crucial for investors to understand logistics' fundamentals and assessment criteria to orient themselves within the current and future dynamics to invest.
How – conceptually?	**How – practically?**
• Research strategy according to the methods acquired in the module SR01 Scientific Research – Qualitative research approach • Lectures in the module IF03 Real Estate Investment and Finance • IFZ Conference: Real Estate Investment and Asset Management 2021 • RICS and HLSU Webinar: Investments in Logistics and Light Industrial	• Academic research for literature review • Conduct interviews with eight experts from the industry by applying an interview guide[1] • Data analysis by applying an evaluation grid[2] and comparing the results to the literature review • Conclusion and critical reflection

1 The interview guide will be explained on page 10 (Interviews – Data Collection & Analysis).
2 The evaluation grid will be explained on page 11 (Interviews – Data Collection & Analysis).

Interviews – Sampling Strategy

Purposive sampling is conducted for this research. In qualitative research, purposive samplings are most frequently considered. Purposive sampling is favorable in allowing access to a wide range of individuals relevant to the research question. This ensures that different perspectives and activities are considered (Bell, Bryman, & Harley, 2018, p. 389).

To ensure an all-around view, three kinds of parties are considered for the interviews. The parties can be categorized into *institutional investors, fund providers,* and *operators/3rd parties.* Each category is represented by at least one expert from the industry. Some experts might speak from the perspective of two categories (e.g., fund provider and investor).

Table 2: **Interviews – Sampling Strategy**

Categories	Inclusion Criteria	Inclusion Reason
Investors	Institutional investors/investment professionals who invest in logistics across Europe	To get the opinions of investors on the European logistics market
Fund Providers	Fund providers who give investors access to logistics investments across Europe	To get the opinions of fund providers on the European logistics market
Operators/ 3rd Parties	Neutral in the logistics investment field (no specific criteria)	To consider diverse perspectives from operators/3rd parties

Interviews – Data Collection & Analysis

To structure the area of research, a guide for the semi-structured interviews according to Bell, Bryman, and Harley (2018) was developed. The interview guide ensures the comparability of the interviews. Furthermore, semi-structured interviews, allow the interviewer to ask follow-up questions or change the order of the questions. The interview guide contains a total of 14 questions, of which 6 questions (blue section: 1a–3b) are on the current situation of the European logistics market and 8 questions (green section: 4a–7b) are on the future of the European logistics market.

For the subsequent data analysis, the interviews are conducted via Microsoft Teams with video transmission or sound recording. All interviewees are asked for their explicit consent to being recorded and they are informed of the study's context. The experts conducted the interview independently of each other. The form of evaluation of the interviews is explained in the next section. The following experts were selected based on the defined sampling strategy (in alphabetical order of the last name):

Table 3: **Overview of Interviewees**

No.	Interviewee	Company	Background
01	Prof. Dr. Thomas Beyerle (T.B.)	Catella Property Valuation GmbH	Managing Director & Head of Group Research
02	Martin Haller (M.H.)	SBB Cargo AG	Chairman of the board at Basel Gateway Nord
03	Bodo Hollung MRICS (B.H.)	LIP Invest GmbH	Shareholder & Managing Director
04	Thomas Karmann (T.K.)	AXA Investment Managers	Global Head of Logistics
05	Thorbjørn Pedersen (T.P.)	Swiss Life Asset Managers Nordics AS	CIO
06	Björn Pfeiffer (B.P.)	Mayfair Capital Investment Management Ltd	Portfolio Manager of the European Industrial & Logistics (EIL) Fund
07	Carla Seidel FRICS (C.S.)	Swiss Life Asset Managers DE GmbH	Real Estate Researcher
08	Ingo Steves (I.S.)	BEOS Logistics GmbH	Managing Partner

The analysis is then carried out in an evaluation grid (see Appendix A: Evaluation Grid). Each interview is organized within the table with the key statements in the respective columns. The statements are then compared and grouped into common themes. Thereafter, the similarities and differences are highlighted and summarized (Guest, MacQueen, & Namey, 2012, pp. 9–10).

The analyzed answers to questions 1a–3b (blue section) are covered in Chapter 3: Analysis I – Experts on the Current Situation of European Logistics. The analyzed answers to questions 4a–6a (green section) are covered in

Chapter 4: Analysis II – Experts on the Future of European Logistics. The analyzed answers to questions 7a–7b (green section) are covered in Chapter 5: Investment Guide. Finally, all the findings from the analysis are compared to Chapter 2: Literature Review to ultimately, draw a conclusion, i.e., to answer the defined research questions (see Chapter 1.1: Research Aim & Questions).

2 Literature Review

Chapter 2 captures existing academic literature in the field of European logistics. It is the result of broad and careful secondary research, and a thorough analysis of said research.

2.1 Fundamentals of Logistics

Before diving into the topic of logistics real estate, it is important to first understand real estate in general as an investment class. Real estate as an investment class is often to be found in the portfolios of institutional investors. Investing in real estate can yield high returns, be useful for diversification, and function as a hedge against inflation. Credit Suisse (2021b) expects the historically low-interest rates to rise modestly and the ongoing economic recovery to continue. This environment should be supportive of real estate investments in 2022. Furthermore, the report states that accelerated growth in e-commerce, digitalization, and working from home (WFH) should continue to specifically benefit the logistics sector while further challenging the outlook for office and retail space. With that being said, pandemic-driven structural shifts persist, and logistics real estate is favored as an asset class (Credit Suisse, 2021b).

Some characteristics of logistics real estate are mentioned hereafter. Though, since the focus of this research paper is not on the buildings and localities themselves, but on the investments, the building and location characteristics are only dealt with on a basic level. Nevertheless, investors need to know the fundamentals to, on the one hand, assess investment opportunities, and on the other hand, orientate themselves within the dynamics in the European logistics market. First and foremost, supply chain management must be understood.

T. T. Quach et al., *Logistics Real Estate*, https://doi.org/10.1007/978-3-658-42837-2_2

Supply Chain Management

Modern life depends on the rapid, efficient, and safe movement of a high volume of materials, components, and finished products around the world (Prologis, n.d.). According to the World Trade Organization (2021), world trade was about $17 trillion in 2020. Credit Suisse (2018) summarized these dynamics in its logistics real estate report as follows: "The flow of goods to be handled is enormous and continues to grow at an above-average pace. [...] Online trade, urbanization, and digitalization are the megatrends characterizing the development of this market.".

Before a bar of chocolate reaches the end consumer, there are a series of steps that precede it. As the term implies, the supply chain is a series of interlinked functions, companies, and individuals. Supply chain management is planning and organizing how the distribution of goods and services will make it from manufacturer to consumer. The supply chain starts with those who produce and supply raw materials or components to manufacturers, continues with the logistics firms that move finished goods to warehouses and distribution centers, and concludes with the hand-off to wholesalers and retailers. So, if the supply of cocoa from Guinea is disrupted, a factory in Switzerland cannot produce chocolate bars (Prologis, n.d.).

Supply chain management is considered one of the most important disciplines when doing business in the 21st century – meaning nowadays many companies' success is dependent on effective supply chain management. Supply chains can only function if a series of interconnected systems work in harmony: shipping and transportation, information and management, and security and construction – and for all this to succeed, it demands logistics real estate (Prologis, n.d.).

Logistics Real Estate

The use of logistic properties is primarily triggered by the needs of trade and industry. Logistics properties are integrated into the company's value chain or external logistics service providers are used (outsourcing) (DIWG, 2021, p. 51). Logistics properties are much more heterogeneous and specific than office and residential properties. This is one of the reasons why they are traded with a risk premium. Similarly, the smaller user base, consisting of industrial companies, retailers, and logistics service providers, leads to a more limited third-party usability (CBRE, 2020, p. 4).

Typical logistics properties tend to be decentralized, except last link/urban logistics properties which are located close to or within the city. Also, typical logistics properties are often single-tenanted. In general, logistics has a negative image and does not enjoy much support among the population and politicians – especially locally. However, from the perspective of local politicians, the advantage of the last link/urban logistics is that workforce is needed to operate the logistic property (Gütle, 2021, p. 6).

Generic logistics buildings can be divided into four sub-asset classes:

- Fulfillment Centers
- Distribution Platforms/Warehouses
- Parcel Hubs
- Last Mile Distribution Hubs

Figure 3 on the next page gives an overview of these four categories with their corresponding characteristics and the next section then explains some of the requirements for the location and properties.

Fulfillment Centers
- Size 80,000 up to 200,000 m²
- Several levels of concrete or steel mezzanine
- Central storage area with robots for handling in recent layout versions
- Packing areas in periphery of building with natural light
- Large office component and social premises for high number of employees
- Ground floor usually as cross dock with HGV ramps
- Access to mezzanines or upper floors by cargo lift
- Connection to public transport and large labor pool in local market

Distribution Platforms/Warehouses
- Typical size 10,000 up to 90,000 m²
- Up to 15 % mezzanine behind dock doors
- Ideally not more than 5 % offices
- Sufficient truck parking area
- Minimum height 10 m; ideally 12,20 m for single layer sprinkler system FM
- Floor load min 5 T/m²
- Loading docks 1/900 m²
- Ideal depth 80 m up to 120 m for single sided ramps
- Often also cross dock layout tor side loading area under canopy (automotive)

Parcel Hubs
- Typical size 3,000 up to 15,000 m²
- Up to 25 % office area for commercial teams
- Necessarily cross dock units with depth 40–60 m
- Minimum height 6 m; usually not sprinklered
- Floor load min 3 T/m², large truck parking areas
- Loading docks along whole façade min 1/100 m²
- Possibly two types of loading docks for HGV and vans
- Location at motorway/highway crossing with 24/7 access

Last Mile Distribution Hubs
- Typical size 3,000 up to 10,000 m²
- Up to 25 % office area for commercial teams
- HGV docks at front side of building
- Level access doors or van docks at long side of building
- Floor load min 3 T/m²
- Loading docks along whole façade min 1/100 m²
- Large van parking areas with electric loading points
- Location in proximity of end customers for last mile distribution with small vehicles (electric vans, bikes etc.)

Figure 3: **Logistics Real Estate – The 4 Sub-Asset Classes** (AXA Investment Managers, 2022)[3]

3 Graphics: Fullfillment Center (AO Architects, 2022), Distribution Platforms/Warehouses (Biz Choice, 2022), Parcel Hubs (Supply Chain Digital, 2020), Last Mile Distribution Hubs (Metapack, 2022)

Requirements for the Location & Property

The macro- and micro-location, the plot, and the property itself play an important role in the requirements. Regarding macro-location the property should be in a logistics region or conurbation, in proximity to a production site, and have optimal transport connection (road, wail, water, air). Ideal micro-location characteristics are, e.g., good infrastructure nearby and on-site (petrol station, retail trade, gastronomy, hotel, etc.), generous street fronts for entrances and exits, few traffic lights, and no residential area in the neighborhood (DIWG, 2021, p. 53).

The plot itself should be at least 2 ha with a rectangular cut (optimal 130–150m, 200–400m). Typically, 40–60% of the land is covered by buildings. Furthermore, a level plot i.e., no incline is ideal. Of course, the development of traffic and technical (water, electricity, gas, telecommunications), protection against force majeure (floods, storms, etc.), as well as fencing (barriers, alarm systems, video surveillance, etc.) are required. The plot should also have enough parking spaces/waiting areas for the trucks and ideally have expansion areas (DIWG, 2021, p. 54).

A very important requirement is the extensive usage permit (at least from 6 am to 10 pm, seven days per week) which heavily depends on the noise and air protection regulations in the area. The construction itself typically has a minimum size of 10,000m^2 and is a single-story hall with a mezzanine in the docking area for office use. Typical for the construction of logistics buildings are concrete and flat sole, waterproofed floor surface, and a flat pitched roof. Also, to be considered are the special requirements regarding the equipment of the building, e.g., the heating, lighting, water, gas, and electricity connection (depending on the use of the building). Moreover, a fire alarm system, sprinkler system, protection in front of the loading gates, and weather aprons must be considered (DIWG, 2021, pp. 54–55).

2.2 Drivers of Logistics

The past years have accelerated and highlighted some existing trends but have also shown new emerging trends. Cushman & Wakefield (2021) define five key drivers that are influencing and driving the logistics real estate market. Understanding these drivers is important to relate how logistics properties fit into the bigger picture of the economy and environment. The five key drivers according to Cushman & Wakefield are:

- Supply Chain Evolution
- Last Link / Urban Logistics
- E-Commerce & Technology
- Sustainability
- Labor

Supply Chain Evolution

The resilience of supply chains is being tested as companies expand globally and therefore, need to hold stock and demand for decentralized networks (Prologis, 2021, p. 4). The biggest change occupiers anticipate as a result of the pandemic is the shortening, or reshoring, of supply chains, which has helped to drive demand for logistics space to record levels. Likewise, Brexit-induced delays have been amplified due to increasingly stringent border checks and customs declarations, requiring more time for mainland European companies to adjust to new arrangements. Companies are seeking to hold more inventory to mitigate risk which in turn increases demand for logistics space. Astonishingly, 46% of European occupiers anticipate that they will increase their warehouse floor space over the next 12 months, among the highest in the online retail sector (Savills, 2022, p. 3).

All these factors coupled with a rising consumer class are driving the need for more logistics space (Prologis, 2021, p. 4). During the Covid-19 lockdowns, online retail in Europe particularly showed the same growth in online sales volume in one year as in the previous five years combined. The online retail revolution is certainly not a new trend but one that has been seeing some of the biggest shifts in the industry and a trend that will continue to shape the sector in the future (Bruer, 2021).

The disruption of the food supply chain being an emerging trend, has shown the ways in and from which places food is sourced – basically the production and distribution of food. The focus is on the localization of food sourcing and on geopolitical factors such as changing trade relationships. Meaning the flow of food from production locations is changing for some markets. In manufacturing and production, technology is playing a major role. In response to recent disruptions, businesses are considering how they hold stock – just-in-time logistics or holding greater inventory levels to maintain supply without interruption. Therefore, facilities closer to the markets with the right operational needs for users to operate effectively and efficiently, are in great demand (Bruer, 2021).

One solution that helps companies manage the ever-more-complicated supply chains is new technologies such as artificial intelligence (AI)-based supply chain management (McKinsey & Company, 2021). Technology and innovation are already contributing to efficiencies and safety in both production and finished goods. Manufacturers can use new technologies to enhance supply chain visibility, improve speed to market, reduce labor reliance, reshore production, and create jobs through relocation. Manufacturing technologies and innovations include automation, 3D and additive printing, Big Data, nanomaterials, autonomous trucks and delivery vehicles, advanced robotics, and artificial intelligence (Cushman & Wakefield, 2018).

More importantly, supply chains are increasingly viewed as a competitive advantage. For companies, the revenue-generation benefits from being able to meet consumer demands regarding product availability, choice, and delivery speed, greatly outweigh the additional real estate costs. Another solution, therefore, is to locate closer to consumers. Locating closer to the consumer also reduces transportation costs, which account for about 50% of supply chain costs. Therefore, the next trend of last link/urban logistics is getting more into focus (Prologis, 2021, p. 4).

Last Link / Urban Logistics

One of the biggest drivers facing logistics users and the property industry is urban and last link logistics. Last link/urban logistics in particular was the focus of investors, and activity in this area has increased since the outbreak of the pandemic (UBS Asset Management, 2020, p. 4). Despite the Covid-19 pandemic, expectations are that people will continue to live more and more in cities. By 2030 over three-quarters of the people of Europe are expected to be living in urban areas and there are expected to be 74 cities with a million people or more across Europe. With increasing challenges to move goods around cities – from the known problem of traffic congestion to emerging restrictions on the types of vehicles moving around cities – it is no wonder that last link logistics is gaining more importance (Bruer, 2021).

E-Commerce & Technology

Consumer expectations have increased permanently, favoring convenience, choice, reliability, and immediacy. These consumer expectations in combination with new digital options have boosted the adoption of e-commerce. E-commerce, as a proportion of retail goods sold globally, grew to nearly 20% in 2020 from about 4% in 2011 (Prologis, 2021, p. 2).

Globally, e-commerce penetration increased at an outsized rate of 390 basis points in 2020, equal to roughly five years of adoption (Prologis, 2021) (see Figure 4: Global E-Commerce Sales and Penetration Rate). In addition, JLL (2020) expects e-commerce sales could hit $1.5 trillion by 2025 which would increase the demand for logistics and industrial space to an additional 1 billion m^2. In the context of logistics real estate, tenants desire sufficient

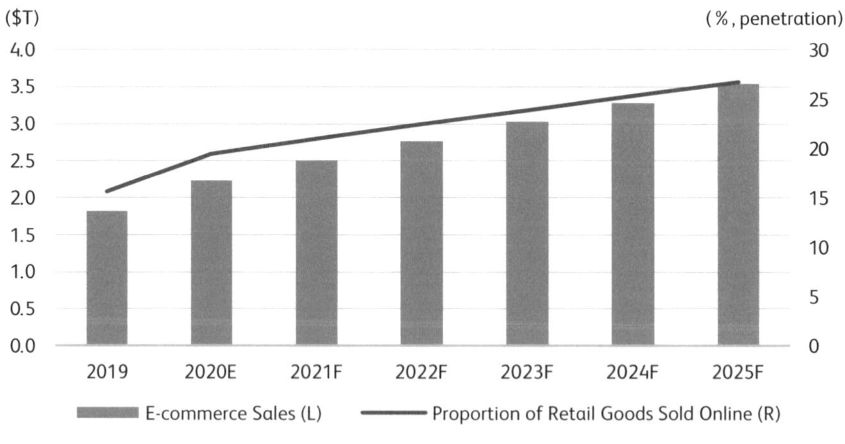

Figure 4: **Global E-Commerce Sales and Penetration Rate** (Prologis, 2021)

space, both in the form of XXL warehouses and smaller last-mile facilities near city centers. The permanence of this shift is debatable, but the evidence suggests that users do not see it as merely temporary. In Q2 2020, the UK logistics market, e.g., saw record turnover, with e-commerce-related functions accounting for the major share (UBS Asset Management, 2020, p. 4).

The implementation of technology is not a new trend. The driver is the broader and wider adoption of technology in and around logistics, as well as throughout the delivery side such as last-link deliveries with robots. Moreover, the collection and use of data from and within logistics buildings, throughout the supply chain, and delivery process are big drivers. Important to remember is that most of the technology in warehouses is used to complement and enhance human skills, efficiency, and productivity. They also make workplaces safer and more accurate. One of the reasons that technology is about to be more widely adopted, is because it is becoming cheaper and more flexible. This greater implementation of technology is not only shaping how buildings look and function, but also the demand for energy usage. This creates pressure on logistics real estate providers to deliver facilities that work now and in the future (Bruer, 2021).

Prologis' study (2021, p. 2) further shows the influence of technology in connection with demographic change. Millennials, the digital natives, comprise 23% of the global population. They have entered higher income brackets and are, therefore, a primary target for retailers. Furthermore, over the past decade, about 2 billion people gained internet access. The internet as a platform for commerce continues to expand around the world. Technology links to the next big driver which is sustainability.

Sustainability

Arguably sustainability is potentially the one that has the greatest impact on the logistics industry. People and businesses have become more focused on sustainability factors and therefore, sustainability is considered a megatrend (AXA Investment Managers, 2021, p. 12).

Sustainability factors must be keenly integrated into businesses and their identities. Moreover, sustainability makes a difference in how people choose to work and the companies they choose to work for. Therefore, potentially it reflects how businesses work, which suppliers they are dealing with, the types of products they store and manufacture, and the types of property companies operate in. More importantly, it is increasingly part of how investors invest their capital (Bruer, 2021).

In the past decade, much of the sustainability features of buildings have been focused on how to reduce carbon emissions through the usage of the buildings. That has been particularly focused on the operating costs of a building. However, the biggest shift that will affect the industry, is how it deals with construction and maintaining the logistics buildings. Logistics buildings account for around 17% of global greenhouse gas emissions. However, 83% of the global greenhouse gas emissions come from the movement of goods by different modes of transport, noticeably from road freight. This means the greatest gains can be made by the mitigation or the reduction of greenhouse gas emissions through the transport side of the logistics industry (Bruer, 2021).

Labor

When it comes to cost, labor is an important driver (Cushman & Wakefield, 2019). Logistics is still a human capital-intensive business. Lots of people are typically required to operate within logistics buildings. However, there are long-standing and significant challenges around the recruitment of appropriate staff, particularly in skilled jobs but also in jobs where it is in general difficult to recruit people. This has a knock-on effect on cost. Therefore, staff retention and performance are important to businesses occupying logistics facilities. Employers are increasingly looking at ways to attract, retain staff, and improve productivity. This has an impact on the type of space they require and how they use it. This includes what goes on inside buildings, e.g., the inclusion of wellness and welfare space for workers and improved quality of the facilities overall. Moreover, the attractiveness and connectivity of the places play a role. People want to work in places that are nice and that are easy for them to access. This is important for occupiers but also for investors, and developers of logistics space in terms of tenant retention. It is about making sure that those occupiers have the tools in place for them to operate effectively and efficiently (Bruer, 2021).

2.3 European Logistics Market

European logistics take-up reached 40 million m^2 by the end of 2021, marking a record year of leasing activity and 40% ahead of the previous five-year average. Germany (8.6 million m^2), the Netherlands (6.9 million m^2), the UK (5.1 million m^2), and Poland (7.3 million m^2) drove leasing activity, whilst Romania (+63%), France (+63%), and Spain (+62%) performed the strongest against their five-year averages (Savills, 2022, p. 3).

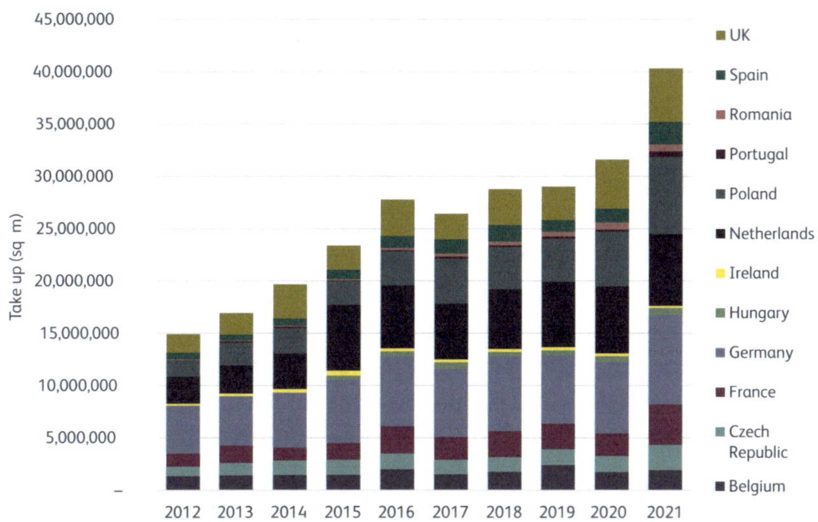

Figure 5: **European Logistics Take-up** (Savills, 2022, p. 3)

Prologis (2017) conducted a survey on Europe's most desirable logistics locations. The report identified five factors that shape location selection in Europe:

- Proximity to major consumption centers
- Regulatory environment
- Labor availability
- Transportation infrastructure
- Total costs/value proposition

In all five categories, the following countries perform well: Germany, Netherlands, Belgium, UK, France, Poland, as well as *other CEE* which include the Czech Republic, Slovakia, Hungary, Romania, and Turkey (Prologis, 2017, pp. 1–2).

The research shows that immediate access to major consumption centers is vital. Meaning access to the gateways of global trade, economic networks, and workforce are the most important location criteria for logistics operators. Furthermore, major population centers with the highest consumption are increasingly important. Metropolitan areas like London, Paris, Milan, and Berlin perform well because they are close to consumers and support an efficient supply chain. The study also shows that many traditionally more expensive countries and markets including the Netherlands, Germany, Belgium, the UK, and France scored well because supply chains are increasingly viewed as a competitive asset. The final finding reveals the rising importance of labor. With changing demographics and increased levels of value-added services in logistics facilities, the availability of qualified staff has become a structural as well as a cyclical driver in location selection (Prologis, 2017, p. 2).

In 2019, European logistics transaction volumes amounted to € 27.7 billion (+7% to 2018; +230% to 2011). More than 50% of the investment volumes in 2019 were accounted by the UK (19%), France (19%), and Germany (17%). However, regional rankings differed from this high-level trend. Amsterdam/Randstad in the Netherlands was the leading logistics investment market with investments of € 1.3 billion in 2019. And thus, it accounts for one-third of the Dutch logistics market (2019: €3.4 billion). The second and third largest regional investment markets in 2019 were Paris (€0.8 billion) and Rhine-Ruhr (€0.6 billion). These markets both account for a much lower share of their domestic investment markets (France: €5.1 billion; Germany: €4.7 billion), equivalent to 16% and 12%, respectively. This reflects their markets being less clustered and offering greater regional diversification (Swiss Life Asset Managers, 2020a, pp. 5–6).

Catella (2022b) surveyed the transaction volumes of 112 countries in Europe. These individual transaction volumes can be found in Appendix B: Catella Logistics Market Map Europe 2022. However, because a basic understanding of the major logistics market is important for further reading, the following countries are presented in a short profile regarding their logistics market (in no particular order):

- UK
- Netherlands
- Germany
- France
- Poland
- Other CEE
- Italy
- Spain

UK

The UK logistics market is very different from that in continental Europe. The top markets include London and the Midlands, due to their size of customer base. The Midlands is attractive due to its proximity to consumers (the east is better than the west), but also because of its infrastructure and the support that local authorities offer to the logistics industry (Prologis, 2017, p. 3).

Netherlands

As one of the hubs of European trade, the Netherlands is consistently a popular location. The top markets include Venlo, Rotterdam, Amsterdam-Schiphol, and Central Brabant. These markets can be distinguished based on their accessibility to major consumption centers, infrastructure, and the support their communities provide to the logistics industry (Prologis, 2017, p. 3).

Germany

As the economic engine of Europe, Germany is at the top of the logistics hotspot rankings. Germany is the largest logistics market in Europe. It is located in the middle of Europe and therefore, most transport routes go through Germany. With its 83 million population and very well-equipped infrastructure, Germany is one of the most attractive countries for logistics real estate investments. In addition, the lowest volatility of returns is shown in logistics investment in Germany (Hollung, 2022). The population and logistics market are spread across many markets. The top markets include Düsseldorf, Rhine-Ruhr, Central Germany, Frankfurt, Cologne/Bonn, and

Hamburg. Proximity to trade from Northern European ports and onward distribution to other locations in Germany are differentiators, as well as the presence of a large consumer base (Prologis, 2017, p. 3).

France

France is favored by the size of its large economy and the quality of its road infrastructure, but constrained by the labor environment and, in general, by cost-benefit dynamics. Among France's many markets, Paris naturally is a top market due to the size of its market, its established logistics industry, and its labor supply (Prologis, 2017, p. 4).

Poland

Poland's logistics market has grown rapidly since the opening of the country's borders. The growth in industrial activity combined with the growing consumer class means that logistics is driven from both ends of the supply chain. Poland ranks in the top 3 countries in Prologis (2017) study because of its strong value proposition, proximity to Western Europe, and extensive transportation infrastructure. Top markets include Central Poland-Lodz, Krakow, Wroclaw, and Western Poland, each with different combinations of these characteristics (Prologis, 2017, p. 4).

Other CEE

CEE is a relatively young market compared to Western Europe and only became part of the European logistics network in the early 2000s when CEE countries joined the EU. Thus, institutional logistics properties in these markets were built after 2000. Demand in this region is driven by its emerging middle class and final assembly industry. The region offers a pro-growth business environment and low costs, which attracts logistics companies, especially those with a higher labor content, such as light manufacturing or more labor-intensive distribution. Key markets include Bucharest and Prague (Prologis, 2017, p. 4).

Italy

Domestic consumption is the main driver of Italy's sizable economy. Italy has limited links to external economies compared with West Germany and the Benelux countries. As a result, Italy is only conditionally one of the locations when it comes to logistics. Among Italy's many markets, Milan is naturally the top performer due to its economic size and existing infrastructure. A smaller market, Bologna, benefits from its central location, multimodality, and ability to reach a large portion of the Italian population (Prologis, 2017, p. 4).

Spain

Similar to Italy, Spain is a large and established economy but has lower connectivity to global economic activity, trade, and links to other major population centers. Madrid is the preferred location, as it is a large population center with a favorable market environment and good infrastructure (Prologis, 2017, p. 4).

2.4 Investments in Logistics Real Estate

European logistics investment reached a record €62 billion in 2021, a 79% increase on the five-year average. The UK (€19.5 billion) boosted volumes, marking a record year, accounting for 31% of activity, whilst Germany (€8.6 billion), France (€6.5 billion) and Sweden (€5.8 billion), and the Netherlands (€5.7 billion) also recorded strong levels of activity (see Figure 6: European Logistics Investment Volumes). Logistics accounted for 66% of European omnichannel investment in 2021, up from 47% in 2019, as investors were willing to pay premiums to gain exposure to the sector and are now becoming less sensitive to location. According to RCA, logistics sales and leaseback transactions have risen by 115% against the five-year average (Savills, 2022, p. 5).

The current European prime rent averages at €5.81/m^2, ranging from €3.75/m^2 in Zaragoza (a city in Spain) to €16.40/m^2 in London. Since Catella's last study in October 2021, prime rents for logistics have risen by an average of almost 3% across all 112 markets surveyed. Due to the sustained investor interest in the logistics segment, yield compression can be observed across all markets. The European average yield is now 4.68% which is 30 basis points lower compared to Catella's last study. The lowest net initial yields, which speak for the most expensive logistics locations in Europe, can be found in the German A locations (3.00%-3.40%) as well as in Venlo (a city in the Netherlands, 3.20%), Paris (3.2,0%), and London (3.00%). The current strong demand for logistics properties can also be seen in the transaction volume within individual countries. For example, a logistics transaction volume

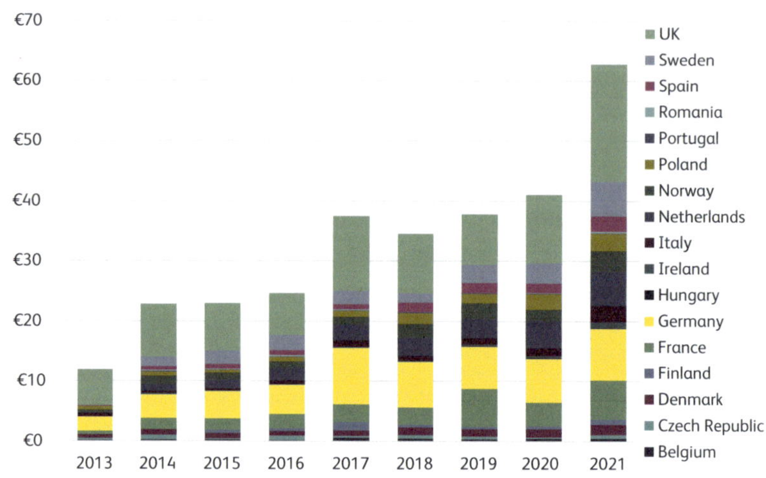

Figure 6: **European Logistics Investment Volumes** (Savills, 2022, p. 5)

of €9.6 billion was recorded in Germany, and a volume of €19.7 billion in the UK, which represents a record value in both cases. In total, an investment volume of around €60 billion was recorded across the markets surveyed, which also represents a new record transaction volume at the European level (Catella, 2022a). The individual prime yield, prime rent, as well as transaction volumes of the 112 surveyed countries can be found in Appendix B: Catella Logistics Market Map Europe 2022 (Catella, 2022b).

Savills research report from February 2022 shows roughly the same picture of yield compression with an average prime yield of 4.20% for European logistics. All surveyed countries moved in 25–50 basis points compared to six months ago (Q2 2021). The UK and Romania were the only markets to remain stable (see Figure 7: European Prime Logistics Yields) (Savills, 2022, p. 5).

Value add investors are now turning their attention to secondary assets to ride the yield wave. Average secondary yields hardened by 34 basis points over the past six months, with Germany and Ireland compressing by 89 basis points and 75 basis points, respectively. Despite rising development costs, the yield spread between new development and the existing stock continues

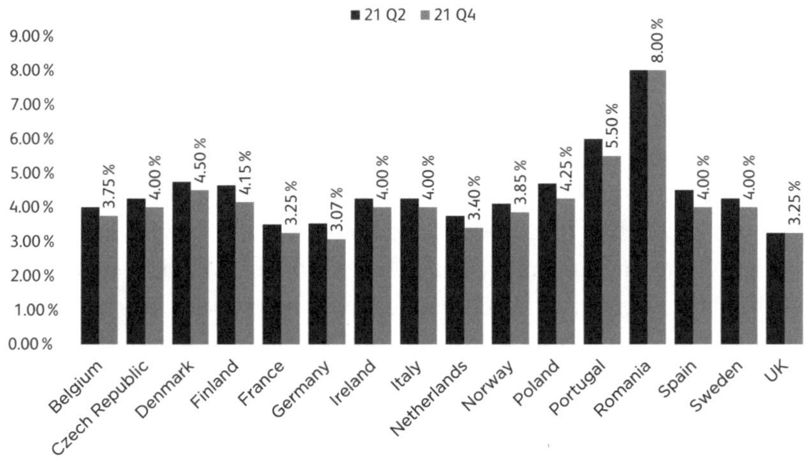

Figure 7: **European Prime Logistics Yields** (Savills, 2022, p. 6)

to close, below 100 basis points in some instances. Land prices continue to rise in major urban areas too, adding upwards pressure on capital values. Capital allocations towards the logistics sector remain strong, and despite rising construction costs, speculative development in the sector is anticipated to rise during 2022/23 as investors move up the risk curve in search of higher returns. Therefore, it is also anticipated that there is still further room for yields to move in for the best stock, particularly in non-core locations (Savills, 2022, pp. 5–6).

That investments in logistics are booming, can also be seen in the launch of various logistics funds in recent years. To give the reader a small insight into investment solutions in European logistics, three funds that invest in European logistics are briefly presented. The funds were not selected according to any criteria – except that they invest in European logistics. These funds are introduced in the following sections:

- Swiss Life ESG European Industrial & Logistics (EIL)
- Swiss Life ESG European Thematic Income & Growth (TIGR)
- Catella Logistik Deutschland Plus

Swiss Life ESG European Industrial & Logistics (EIL)

The Swiss Life Investment Foundation in cooperation with Swiss Life Asset Managers launched an investment solution for European industrial and logistics real estate in September 2020. The fund is targeted at Swiss pension funds and institutional investors looking to invest in a segment with attractive growth prospects. The fund *Swiss Life Real Estate Funds (LUX) S.A., SICAV-SIF – European Industrial & Logistics* invests in a diversified and high-quality portfolio of industrial and logistics real estate in Europe. The focus is on Germany and France but includes properties in the rest of Europe as well, particularly in the UK, Benelux, and Switzerland. Approximately half of the allocation is to industrial and logistics properties (Swiss Life Asset Managers, 2020b). The fund volume comprises €113.3 million (as of 31 December 2020). The target volume is around €1 billion (Corpus Sireo, 2021).

Swiss Life ESG European Thematic Income & Growth (TIGR)

Another fund of Swiss Life Asset Managers that invests in logistics is the *ESG European Thematic Income & Growth* fund. The objective of this fund is to build and manage a long-term-oriented, sustainable European portfolio to acquire core and core+ properties in selected markets. Since its launch in 2019, the fund has grown to over €500 million and currently manages 10 properties in six European countries (Swiss Life Asset Managers, 2022). Together with the European Industrial & Logistics fund, this fund invests in high-quality logistics properties in Germany, France, Italy, and Spain. These properties comprise a total area of 187,967m^2 and a diversified tenant base, with 55% of the portfolio comprising cold storage logistics, which is expected to grow in the coming years. The cities in the portfolio are located along strong logistics routes in established locations (Swiss Life Asset Managers, 2021).

Catella Logistik Deutschland Plus

Another example is the *Catella Logistik Deutschland Plus* fund. This fund invests in sustainable storage and logistics properties in Germany and neighboring countries. The investment focus is on properties in established logistics regions close to transport hubs and conurbations as well as production centers. All locations have solid fundamental data and growth potential in the future in combination with stable cash flow for property acquisition. The investment strategy focuses on existing properties as well as new-build properties and special logistics halls (e.g., parcel distribution centers, delivery centers, fulfillment centers, cross docks, light industrial and industrial properties, refrigerated logistics, etc.). The highest possible capacity for alternative uses and object flexibility as well as multimodal properties/locations (e.g., track siding) are strongly preferred. The investment horizon of the broadly diversified portfolio, which is expected to consist of 18 to 20 properties, is 10 to 12 years. The fund, which is aimed at professional and semi-professional investors, has a target volume of around €350 million (Catella, 2021c).

3 Analysis I – Experts on the Current Situation of European Logistics

3

Understanding the current situation of the European logistic sector is vital to predict how the industry may evolve in the coming years. Therefore, in this chapter, the current situation in the European logistics sector is analyzed. Specifically, experts from the industry give their opinion on the impact of megatrends on the European logistics sector and assess the current investment situation. The results are presented in 3 subchapters: Overview – European Logistics, Megatrends, and Current Investments.

3.1 Overview – European Logistics

In this overview, the experts give their opinion on the current situation in the European logistics sector. In particular, the following question is treated:

1a: How do you assess the current situation in the European logistics sector?

The experts agree that the European logistics sector is currently characterized by a surplus in demand and a shortage of logistics space (Hollung, 2022; Karmann, 2022; Steves, 2022). This is not only evident in the current low vacancy rates. In fact, European logistics vacancy rates fell from 5.1% to 3.5% over the course of 2021 (Savills, 2022, p. 4). Moreover, take-up of logistics space across Europe broke all records in Q4 2021. A total of over 9.9 million m^2 taken in the final quarter pushed full-year totals to over 33.5 million m^2. This is a plus of 35% on the previous year and 50% if compared to the 5-year average (JLL, 2022, p. 2).

Businesses demand more storage space for safety function due to several factors. One of them being an increasingly divided atmosphere among world leaders, particularly the tariffs imposed by the US on China. Plus, rising

T. T. Quach et al., *Logistics Real Estate*, https://doi.org/10.1007/978-3-658-42837-2_3

inflation and labor costs have gradually begun to undermine China's status as the engine of global export markets. Also, the Covid-19 crisis has thrown further factors such as self-sufficiency, digitalization, e-commerce, as well as ESG into focus and drawn more activity back to Europe (UBS Asset Management, 2020, p. 2).

Martin Haller, Chairman of the board at Basel Gateway Nord, points out that after the medical impact of the Covid-19 virus has passed, operators need to rethink how to best supply consumers and businesses as well as how to operate effectively while mitigating the risk of any future major disruptions. Eventually, new requirements for the logistics sector have arisen. This introduces an interesting shift in the concept of global supply chains – which has previously been driven by the factor of cost – the emphasis appears to now be on risk management (Haller, interview, March, 24 2022). This trend is also illustrated by a recent BCG (2021) survey, which found that end-to-end supply chain visibility is the top concern of logistics CEOs. Thomas Karmann, Global Head of Logistics at AXA Investment Managers, reasoned that additional warehouse space is required because companies are holding bigger inventory to prevent supply chain disruption (Karmann, interview, February, 24 2022). In addition, Prologis (2021) argued that there is a shift from a *just-in-time* model to a *just-in-case* model resulting in companies holding about 5–10% more inventory in stock.

Finally, Covid-19 is expected to result in large investments in infrastructure to fiscally stimulate the local market. There have already been several EU-wide projects to invest in road, rail, port, and air infrastructure. If implemented well, this has the potential to increase the efficiency of local networks and integrate more peripheral locations (UBS Asset Management, 2020, p. 3).

Prof. Dr. Thomas Beyerle, Managing Director and Head of Group Research at Catella, concludes that on the one hand, the European logistics sector is a booming market, on the other hand, it is necessary to consider the uncertainties arising from the current political and economic instabilities which lead to risks in the supply chains (Beyerle, interview, April, 4 2022). However, overall, the experts have a positive view of the European logistics sector with the conclusion that the Covid-19 pandemic has increased the need for agility and flexibility. Topics like supply chain diversification/ disruption or onshoring/nearshoring emerge and play an ever-greater role

(Pfeiffer, 2022; Seidel, 2022; Steves, 2022). These and further megatrends are analyzed in the next subchapter.

3.2 Megatrends

Megatrends are a significant driver for the logistics sector. The drivers of logistics real estate have already been launched in the literature review (see Chapter 2.2: Drivers of Logistics). This chapter covers expert opinions on the key megatrends that currently impact the European logistics industry. In particular, the following questions are treated:

2a: What changes do you see in terms of deglobalization, supply chain, or e-commerce?

2b: What is your opinion on urban/last link logistics?

2c: What impact have automatization and electrification on the logistics sector?

The experts' opinions on these questions are presented in the following sections:

- Deglobalization & Supply Chains Resilience
- E-Commerce Penetration
- Last Link Logistics
- Automatization & Electrification

Deglobalization & Supply Chains Resilience

The experts agree that the Covid-19 pandemic highlighted the key role of logistics and the relative resilience of the sector, i.e., sparked the discussions about deglobalization (Haller, 2022; Karmann, 2022; Pfeiffer, 2022; Seidel, 2022). Trade as a share of GDP has been largely stagnant since the global financial crisis, while foreign direct investment has fallen away significantly (UBS Asset Management, 2020, p. 3). This illustrates the current trend of deglobalization. Björn Pfeiffer, Portfolio Manager of the ESG European Industrial & Logistics (EIL) Fund at Mayfair Capital, explains that the trend of deglobalization and onshoring/nearshoring, i.e., bringing production back or closer to the own country, has a significant impact on the European logistics sector. The industry became aware that its trade partners are not always stable. The Russia-Ukraine war is forcing corporates to navigate supply chain disruptions, sanctions, and a humanitarian crisis (Pfeiffer, interview April, 6 2022). Carla Seidel, Real Estate Researcher at Swiss Life Asset Managers, explains that an important question to be answered by the players in the industry is: Which countries have politically authoritarian systems and therefore, are possibly less reliable as a partner for us? Onshoring/nearshoring is heavily discussed at the moment but the reasons in terms of costs, capacity, labor space, etc. which speak for outsourcing, persist until today (Seidel, interview, March, 23 2022). Nevertheless, the geopolitical situation has become an increasingly important driver for the European logistics sector, especially when it comes to supply chains (Haller, 2022).

Supply chains are complex and supply chain management has become significantly more challenging. Longer and increasingly interconnected commodity flows reflect the growing complexity of product portfolios. Moreover, increasing attention to the environmental impact of supply chains is leading to regionalization and optimization of goods flows. As a result, companies, and stakeholders are increasingly focused on supply chain resilience. Most relevant for the sector is identifying the type of accessibility required given the type of goods moving through the supply chain, in addition to their origin and ultimate destination (Cushman & Wakefield, 2018).

E-Commerce Penetration

Extended lockdown periods have continued to support the growth of online retail across Europe. Western Europe's e-commerce penetration rate jumped from an average of 11% to 15% between 2019 and 2020, as retailers adapt their supply chains to cater to changing consumer habits. By this measure, the western European average penetration rate remains around five years behind the growth path observed within the UK, although this is boosted by France, the Netherlands, and Germany. A marginal reduction in annual e-commerce penetration growth rate is anticipated as several restrictions have been lifted, although some consumer habits will remain. In the UK, online retail sales as a % of total retail sales rose from 28% to 29% between 2020 and 2021, despite the expectation that the removal of lockdowns could see

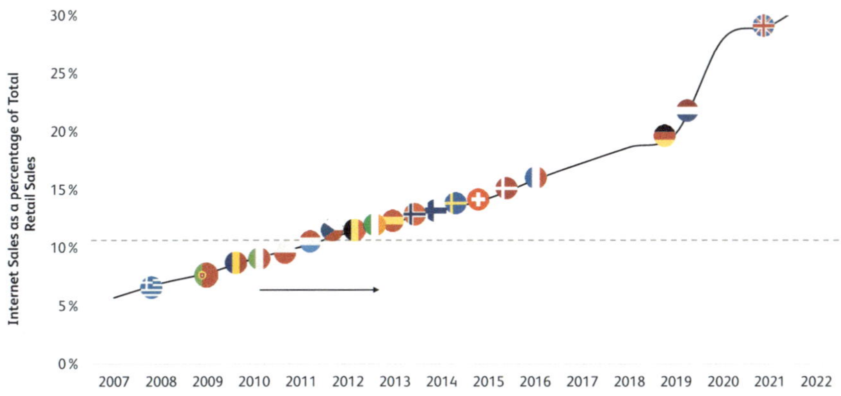

Figure 8: **European E-commerce Penetration Rate by Country** (Savills, 2022, p. 2)

e-commerce spending fall (see Figure 8: European E-commerce Penetration Rate by Country, 2021). It is expected that the average Western European e-commerce penetration will hover around 15–18% (Savills, 2022, p. 2).

Since the onset of the pandemic, online retail sales have surged across all major European economies. E-commerce drives a greater need for warehouse space in Europe. It is a trend that has been accelerated during the Covid-19 pandemic. This is illustrated by the fact that e-commerce-dedicated logistics space accounted for an estimated 20% of total European take-up in 2021 (Karmann, 2022).

The experts expect that e-commerce penetration will continue because consumer habits are "sticky" once barriers to adoption are overcome (Seidel, 2022). Furthermore, Thorbjørn Pedersen, CIO at Swiss Life Asset Managers Nordics, indicates that innovation and supply chain investments made during or in the wake of the pandemic should increase the competitiveness of online options. This is especially true for segments with low e-commerce penetration before the pandemic such as the food industry. The continuation of e-commerce penetration is leading to sustained demand for logistics space. To illustrate the influence of e-commerce penetration: When you buy something online, it takes three times more storage space than when you buy it in a retail shop directly (Pedersen, interview, April, 5 2022).

Given the pandemic-related restrictions on in-store services and spending, e-commerce growth may temporarily slow, and consumers will want to enjoy the experience of personal shopping, travel, and entertainment again (Karmann, 2022). However, Bodo Hollung, Shareholder & Managing Director of LIP Invest, points out that before the Covid-19 pandemic, a structural shift in retail was already in play. This suggests demand for logistics space will remain high (Hollung, interview, March, 10 2022). Although the demanded logistics space in the European market is likely to see different requirements when compared with traditional industrial uses (Haller, 2022). Due to the high volume of reverse logistics (returns), warehouses need to be generally bigger, have higher specifications, and be more tech-enabled (UBS Asset Management, 2020, p. 5).

Last Link Logistics

Before going into the expert opinions, it is important to clarify the definition of last link logistics once again (see Chapter 1.2: Definition & Delimitation). In the context of e-commerce, *link* in *last link* refers to the connection to the rest of the supply chain, while *last* refers to the end of the supply chain that is reached when the package is delivered. The general rule of thumb for last link facilities is that they should be within a 30-minute drive time of major city centers and as close as possible to the first delivery point (Cushman & Wakefield, 2019).

Bodo Hollung (2022) points out critically that last link refers to distribution centers on the outskirts of the city, from where parcels are transported to the city center to be distributed to the end consumer. For that reason, everything which is 1 km away from the end consumer, are distribution centers or pick-up stations and not "real" logistics properties. The "real" logistics properties e.g., warehouses are located either on the outskirts of the cities or in industrial zones. One way or another, people who order goods online want to have their orders delivered as fast as possible – basically, on-demand. As described in the previous chapter, due to the e-commerce penetration more and more logistics space is required. To meet this need, companies must be as close as possible to the end consumer, i.e., as close as possible to the city. Therefore, last link logistics (or distribution centers and pick-up stations) thrive on the e-commerce trend. Currently, the demand for logistics in an urban setting is higher than the supply. The problem is, as already known, that there is rarely space available – especially not in urban areas (Pfeiffer, 2022).

Parcel service providers are flooding residential areas; each of them with the ultimate goal to reach individual households. Hence, a white-label[4] concept makes no sense from an entrepreneurial point of view. This is, therefore, still an unresolved problem. However, in any case, more space is needed in the city or in peri-urban areas where goods can change from the big container to the small container for the last mile delivery (Haller, 2022). The experts agree that a major transformation in this area will be needed in the future. Possible solutions are to tear down old park houses in the city, deliver by bike, or develop not efficiently used buildings in the urban area into last link logistics (Pfeiffer, 2022). Furthermore, the end consumer plays an important role when it comes to the topic of last link logistics. Last link logistics is influenced by us consumers – we are the last mile by bringing and picking up a package. The rationale behind this is: Since it is just around the corner, I can do it myself. That could possibly be the future of last link logistics (Beyerle, 2022).

Automation & Electrification

To build up and maintain an important role in global supply chains, nowadays it is obvious that logistics providers need to achieve a competitive advantage in terms of digitalization and automation. The history of logistics is also a history of automation, from the steam engine to the forklift to today's robotic pickers and packers. So, today's fevered interest in new machinery, after a lull of several years, has plenty of precedents. Many trends are thrusting automation toward the top of the logistics CEO's agenda, not least these three: a growing shortage of labor, an explosion in demand from online retailers, and some intriguing technological advances. Put it all together, McKinsey (2019) estimates that the transportation-and-warehousing industry has the third-highest automation potential of any sector.

4 A white-label product is a product or service produced by one company (the producer) that other companies (the marketers) rebrand to make it appear as if they had made it. The name derives from the image of a white label on the packaging that can be filled in with the marketer's trade dress. White label products are sold by retailers with their own trademark but the products themselves are manufactured by a third party (Wikipedia, 2021).

Logistics is a labor-intensive business. The high cost of labor and the relatively low cost of capital (to e.g., buy machines or invest in softwares) lead to the trend of automation. Occupiers can reduce the number of employees by replacing them with machines. Especially the big companies invest in automation, since normally, for them it is easier to get cheap financing. In addition, investors are paying more attention to the efficiency of a building from a cargo flow point of view when acquiring an asset (Pedersen, 2022); but more about the investment criteria in Chapter 5: Investment Guide.

Electrification of vehicles is an important trend in the European logistics sector; with good reason because transport accounts for more than 16% of greenhouse gas (GHG) emissions globally and 25% of GHG emissions in the EU. In the pressure to decarbonize logistics, cooperations and alliances are taking off to tackle the decarbonization challenge. A rise in sustainability-related acquisitions and – even more so – in cooperation and alliances to develop cross-industry solutions at the interface of logistics, truck OEMs (Original Equipment Manufacturers), infrastructure companies, energy players, and logistics customers can be observed (pwc, 2022). Sustainable solutions to decarbonize the logistics sector are discussed further in Chapter 4.1: Trends to Watch – ESG.

The change can already be seen today, e.g., with Amazon. Amazon's electric vehicles are already hitting the road since 2021, ahead of tens of thousands of vehicles hitting the road over the next few years (Amazon, 2021). Accordingly, logistics properties must be equipped with charging stations. In countries like, e.g., Germany, Norway, or the UK some transport companies have switched to electric vehicles already when it comes to delivering parcels in the city center (Hollung, 2022; Pedersen, 2022; Pfeiffer, 2022).

The common mindset that logistics is per se "dirty" is wrong. The well-known shift towards greener cities does not stop at logistics. This can be seen in various cities. E.g., in London, one pays higher taxes when driving a petrol or diesel-powered car instead of an electric car. Since cities have set the goal to become greener and as environmentally friendly as possible, it is getting more attractive for authorities to engage with logistics (Pfeiffer, 2022).

Electric vehicles reduce environmental pollution and cause less noise. However, they do not solve the lack-of-space problem mentioned previously regarding last link logistics. Nevertheless, due to the low noise level of electric vehicles, delivery times could be extended, i.e., packages can be delivered early in the morning until late in the evening. In this way, the delivery trips would be distributed throughout the whole day and there would be fewer traffic jams (Haller, 2022).

3.3 Current Investments

In this chapter, the experts discuss why logistics has become so attractive for investors and give their opinion on the current investment situation in the European logistics real estate market. In particular, the following questions are treated:

3a: Why is logistics becoming increasingly attractive to investors?

3b: How do you assess the current investment situation in the European logistics real estate market?

The question of why investing in logistics real estate is easy to answer if one's own behavior regarding online shopping is observed. The population demands online shopping and to fulfill that need alone, an enormous amount of logistics real estate is required. Simply put, logistics is a resilient product, everybody needs and understands the basic concept of it (Pfeiffer, 2022; Seidel, 2022).

Furthermore, the experts point out that logistics is basically system relevant. This became even more visible with the Covid-19 pandemic (Pfeiffer, 2022; Steves 2022). Though, Bodo Hollung (2022) emphasizes that this asset class was not necessarily pushed by the pandemic alone and nothing remarkable has changed in the supply chains – but some producers considering having more than just one supplier. Hence, a shift was already in play before the pandemic. The Covid-19 pandemic mainly impacted e-commerce, but other than that, European logistics real estate has been attractive for investors as an asset class already before the pandemic.

What also can be observed is that European logistics real estate has changed faster and more extensively over the last few years than offices or residential properties. Investors perceive this transformation and pressure to change ultimately as growth and market potential. As explained in the previous Chapter 3.2: Megatrends, investors moreover, expect the e-commerce trend to further grow and they see potential in the future of this asset class, especially in last link logistics (Pfeiffer, 2022).

Ingo Steves, Managing Partner at BEOS Logistics, explains this asset class has become increasingly attractive to investors most of all due to the following features of logistics real estate (Steves, interview, April, 1 2022):

- Stable cash flows
- Low CapEx (Capital Expenditure)
- Manageable asset management capacity
- Transparent product that is easy to understand globally
- High liquidity
- Good credit rating of tenants
- Long-term and straightforward contracts (underwriting)
- Low vacancies and tenant retention rate at almost 100%
- Rental growth potential
- Rapid implementation (construction), the pipeline can be stopped quickly (e.g., in crises)

When it comes to the assessment of the current investment situation in the European logistics real estate market, the experts fully agree that the market is characterized by high competition with loads of players and transactions (Hollung, 2022; Pfeiffer, 2022; Steves 2022). Furthermore, logistics real estate in Europe has shown the strongest rental growth in 2021 in over two decades. JLL's European logistics rental index (excluding Russia) rose 8.6% YoY in 2021, as robust occupier demand coupled with low vacancy and rising land prices, pushed up rental levels across the board (JLL, 2022, p. 3).

The attractiveness of this asset class can also be seen in the declining cap rates and the higher volumes traded. In fact, prime logistics yields continued to fall in many key European markets in Q4 2021. Expectations of rental growth, low-interest rates, and strong investor demand are forecast to push yields even lower (Karmann, 2022; Steves, 2022).

At the moment the pressure to invest can also be seen in eased investment criteria of some investors. Instead of logistics properties, some investors settle for light industrial real estate because those are easier to get currently. Bodo Hollung (2022) describes this settlement for alternative properties as "dilution" of the asset class logistics.

3.4 Interim Summary – Current Situation of European Logistics

The current situation of the European logistics sector has been analyzed in this chapter. This subchapter gives a brief interim summary of the first part of the analysis: Experts on the Current Situation of European Logistics.

According to the experts, the Covid-19 crisis highlighted the key role played by logistics and the relative resilience of the sector. The current situation in the European logistics market is characterized by a surplus in demand. The shortage of logistics space is reflected in the low vacancy rates. In fact, European logistics vacancy rates fell from 5.1% to 3.5% over the course of 2021. Moreover, take-up of logistics space across Europe broke all records in Q4 2021. A total of over 9.9 million m^2 taken in the final quarter pushed full-year totals to over 33.5 million m^2.

Additionally, an increase in e-commerce and supply chain reconfiguration should continue to boost demand for logistics space, especially in urban areas. In combination with constrained supply, this is forecast to continue to push up prime rents. Logistics real estate in Europe has shown the strongest rental growth in 2021 in over two decades. JLL's European logistics rental index rose 8.6% YoY in 2021. Nevertheless, with the Russia-Ukraine war and the uncertainties that come with it, new requirements in terms of flexibility and agility for the European logistics sector have arisen. In summary, demographic, economic, and technological megatrends, as well as political risks are currently driving supply chain planning in the logistics market.

When it comes to the assessment of the current investment situation in the European logistics real estate market, the experts fully agree that the market is characterized by high competition, declining cap rates, and high transaction volumes. However, European logistics real estate as an asset class is expected to remain of considerable interest to investors due to its stable cash flows, low CapEx, simplicity/manageability, high liquidity, tenants with good credit ratings, and rental growth potential.

Ultimately, expectations of rental growth, low-interest rates, and strong investor demand coupled with continued low vacancy are forecasted to push yields even lower. How will the journey of European logistics continue? The experts will give their opinion on the future of European logistics in the next Chapter 4: Analysis II – Experts on the Future of European Logistics.

4 Analysis II – Experts on the Future of European Logistics

4

Now that the current situation of European logistics has been analyzed, this chapter focuses on the future of European logistics. Experts predict how the industry may evolve in the coming years. They specifically shed light on climate-, environmental- and social aspects, as well as the opportunities and challenges investors should look out for in the future. Considering these trends, opportunities, and challenges the experts then give a market outlook for future investments in European logistics. The results are presented in 3 subchapters: Trends to Watch – ESG, Opportunities & Challenges, and Market Outlook.

4.1 Trends to Watch – ESG

At the latest now, one can say that ESG has risen quite high on the agenda of many investors and therefore, is a trend to watch out for when it comes to the future of European logistics. In this section, the experts discuss the path to sustainable logistics. In particular, the following questions are treated:

4a: Where do you see the future of logistics between environmental protection, social aspects, and digital solution?

4b: How does the path to sustainable logistics look like?

4c: As an investor, how important is what is happening within the space? Are you providing financing for automation/improvements?

The recent pandemic has sharpened the ESG debate, as we have observed how nature thrived during the lockdowns and reduced production has led to notably lower emissions in most major global cities. While many operators have managed to avoid this issue for many years, the growth in ESG-focused funds will most likely lead to increased pressure and eventually material

T. T. Quach et al., *Logistics Real Estate*, https://doi.org/10.1007/978-3-658-42837-2_4

discounts on any company seen to be not keeping up (UBS Asset Management, 2020, p. 5).

The experts agree that ESG is not a new topic in the logistics sector. The substantive topics around sustainability have been around decades ago and appear today under the name of ESG. ESG has become a key factor in every asset class – consequentially, also in European logistics real estate. This is not only evident in the increasing importance of ESG certifications when it comes to investment vehicles, but also in the increasing importance of modern logistics (Hollung, 2022; Karmann, 2022; Pedersen, 2022; Pfeiffer, 2022; Seidel, 2022; Steves, 2022).

The transformation of the logistics market is expected to be faster than in the office or residential market since the pressure on the logistics industry is greater. Especially, the EU taxonomy[5] will put a lot of pressure on European logistics real estate (Beyerle, 2022).

Regarding the *environment* side of ESG, it will remain difficult to get new land zoned for logistics use. The people who live in the area have to be convinced that the environmental impact of a logistics building is very limited or even positive. Therefore, emission-free/carbon-neutral logistics buildings, e.g., wooden constructions are high in demand (Karmann, 2022). When it comes to possible solutions toward more sustainable logistics, the experts mention the following examples: electrifications of vehicles, on-site renewables, efficient sealing of the surface, solar panels, LED lighting, carbon-neutral constructions, using recycled materials, and air- or groundwater heat pumps (Hollung, 2022; Pfeiffer, 2022; Steves, 2022).

The growth in green energy has created new opportunities for landlords. Logistics warehouses, e.g., are very well suited to solar panels, due to their large flat shape. As a result, industry sources have suggested that fitting large warehouses with solar panels – either to sell to tenants or sell back to the

5 The EU taxonomy for sustainable activities (i.e. "green taxonomy") is a classification system established to clarify which investments are environmentally sustainable, in the context of the European Green Deal. The aim of the taxonomy is to prevent greenwashing and to help investors make greener choices. Investments are judged by six objectives: climate change mitigation, climate change adaptation, the circular economy, pollution, effect on water, and biodiversity. The taxonomy came into force in July 2020 (Wikipedia, 2022a).

grid – can be highly accretive to returns. Even if these subsidies end, the growth in green-oriented fund management is likely to see carbon-neutral warehouses attract a decent premium in capital markets (UBS Asset Management, 2020, p. 5).

Martin Haller (2022) points out that the reduction of CO_2 emissions is a current trend. However, natural value and biodiversity also play a significant role when it comes to sustainability. Meaning the plausibility assessment of land use, the replacement of destroyed natural value, as well as the increase of the natural value of the land, will become more crucial in the future. The problem is that the natural value is more complex to measure than the CO_2 emission plus, there is still too little awareness when it comes to the impact of biodiversity.

Regarding the *social* side of ESG, warehouses typically rely on large pools of labor. New jobs can be created in the logistics sector by developing new large-format schemes in areas of high unemployment. There is a chance automation may limit this somewhat, although in the short-term it is likely that labor will still be important for most occupiers (UBS Asset Management, 2020, p. 5). More importantly, logistics will remain a physical business in the future, simply because certain things cannot be replaced digitally. Automation and digitalization, therefore, have their limits. Another point that must be considered is that digitalization can also be bad for the environment, as it leads to more individuality, e.g., more online orders which have to be transported. This again has a bad impact on the environment (Haller, 2022).

Regarding the *governance* side of ESG, topics like employee well-being and reasonable company management have shifted into focus. Securing employees for the logistics business is getting more and more important. Thomas Karmann (2022) showcases the importance with the following numbers: Out of the total costs of the supply chain, 10% is rent-, 30% is labor-, 30% is inventory-, and 30% is transport cost. Labor cost is three times the rent costs and therefore, should be much more critical to the occupiers. It is important to consider how to attract labor in a certain area and how to create a good work environment to secure the workforce. This is not only a significant criterion for occupiers but also for investors.

To emphasize the importance of ESG in logistics, the ESG strategy of AXA Investment Managers (AXA IM) is briefly presented. AXA IM has set the following ESG strategy (AXA IM, n.a.):

- Target BREEAM[6] Excellent certification on all new developments
- BREEAM Very Good as target for the upgrade of existing assets
- Refinancing strategy by Green Bonds requiring certification
- Innovation for employee retention: WELL Building standard
- Reletting strategies focus on Improvement of energy efficiency

Thomas Karmann (2022) adds that AXA IM rather invests in their logistics building, e.g., by installing LED lighting, upgrading the cantina or locker rooms for the occupier's employees than giving cash incentives, e.g., rent-free periods to the tenant. This way a better work environment within the building is created and at the same time, the investments create value for AXA IM as an investor.

But not every investor provides financing for automation or improvements of the inner life of their logistics buildings. LIP Invest, e.g., only acquires the asset and invests in the construction itself, i.e., the outer shell of the property; and everything concerning the inner life is the responsibility of the user (Hollung, 2022). Another example is, Swiss Life Asset Managers, which owns the buildings, and the tenants own the machinery. The advantage here is that the tenant's machinery usually lasts longer than the lease contracts. In that case, the tenant will most likely want to prolong the lease contract (Pedersen, 2022). However, Swiss Life Asset Managers includes a budget for refurbishments, tenant improvements, and ESG investments into its business plan when acquiring an asset. The building technology is not a "scope of work" for the investor since it is usually not the investors' core competency. Hence, investors focus on the floor and the façade, i.e., the logistics building as such. The building service and software, which refer to the supply chain or the operation, generally stay the responsibility of the occupier (Pfeiffer, 2022).

6 BREEAM (Building Research Establishment Environmental Assessment Method), first published by the Building Research Establishment (BRE) in 1990, is the world's longest established method of assessing, rating, and certifying the sustainability of buildings. More than 550,000 buildings have been BREEAM-certified and over two million are registered for certification in more than 50 countries worldwide (Wikipedia, 2022b).

Nevertheless, at the end of the day, the tenant and his employees need to be happy and healthy to stay in the building. This means investors eventually have to scan every asset based on ESG criteria. For the future, it can be said that in such a competitive market, all ESG questions must be answered crystal-clear (Pfeiffer, 2022; Steves, 2022).

4.2 Opportunities & Challenges

To predict a market outlook for the European logistics sector, it is necessary to look at the opportunities and challenges that will face the industry in the future. In this section, the experts discuss the potential and key issues that will drive the future of logistics real estate. In particular, the following questions are treated:

5a: What opportunities and challenges will drive the future of logistics real estate?

5b: How will the logistics industry rise to such challenges?

First, the experts agree that there is still a lot of potential for investors in the European logistics market. This is due to several opportunities which will be discussed now. The simplest and probably most important point is that logistics is basic infrastructure; it is not like a shopping mall or a fancy office building. Therefore, macroeconomic risks do not play a major role when it comes to investments in logistics real estate. Furthermore, as discussed earlier, the experts predict that e-commerce penetration will continue which also represents a big opportunity for the logistics sector. Thorbjørn Pedersen (2022) further explains, many firms who are operating in old facilities now are going to need new facilities sooner or later because new facilities are more economical. This in turn creates new investment opportunities since the old facilities can be completely renovated or even demolished and a new logistics building can be created on that land plot. Of course, additional potential comes with the discussed megatrends like last link logistics and ESG. Regarding ESG, investors can, e.g., add a green premium when buying an asset (Pfeiffer, 2022). Thomas Karmann (2022) implies that from an investor's perspective, there are hardly any concerns when it comes to the fundamental drivers influencing the European logistics market. And to emphasize once again, as an investor, logistics real estate in Europe represents a very liquid product that poses a low risk and, on the other hand, offers great potential in an emerging market with rental price growth (Karmann, 2022; Pfeiffer, 2022; Steves, 2022).

Despite all the opportunities, some issues still exist. The Covid-19 crisis is at an advanced stage and a way out of the crisis is visible, however with lingering uncertainty. One fact is that Asia and the US have recovered faster from the economic shock due to the pandemic than Europe (pwc, 2021, p. 11). The pandemic has not yet been finally overcome and in addition, huge uncertainties come with the Russia-Ukraine war. Due to the Russia-Ukraine war, the transport routes through Russia are interrupted which is probably the most incisive development for the logistics sector. There is a possible risk that European logistics funds will suffer due to their investments in countries close to Russia (e.g., Poland, the Czech Republic, Slovenia, and Hungary). Furthermore, investors have to take interest rate development into account. As a result, it is also taking longer for confidence to return and investment activity to pick up in Europe (Hollung, 2022).

But let us start with the basic challenges in logistics. Basically, nobody wants logistics in front of their doorstep. So, the challenging question is, how to get the maximum use of logistics in a conurbation in the first place? Another problem logistics is facing is that this industry is hardly creating new jobs – which does not make the plausibility of a new logistics building in an urban area easier (Beyerle, 2022).

There is and will be a high dynamism in the European logistics market. However, the logistics industry is not known as a highly innovative sector. The fact that it is an industry with a low margins business, especially when it comes to transport logistics and the physical movement of goods, makes things even more challenging (Haller, 2022).

To master the mentioned challenges, the experts agree that the logistics industry must become more efficient through innovation, quickly adapt to change, and develop holistic thinking towards ESG. In particular, the optimization of transport routes must be a priority in the future. To boost this transformation process, the governments and authorities must be cooperative as well, i.e., have an open mind towards logistics. Only this way the excess demand in European logistics can be met in the future (Beyerle, 2022; Steves, 2022).

In summary, although there are a lot of opportunities in investing in European logistics real estate, there are still some key issues to face. A lot of discipline will be required in the future since investment opportunities become increasingly rare and investors are under pressure to deploy money. Hence, investing in the right assets in this highly competitive market is arguably the biggest challenge for investors (Karmann, 2022; Pfeiffer, 2022).

4.3 Market Outlook

In 2020 the Covid-19 pandemic held the world's economies hostage which led to record-breaking declines in economic activity. This situation would normally not be favorable to occupier demand or investor appetite, but this was not the case for the European logistics sector. However, what will the future of European logistics look like? Based on the trends to watch, as well as the opportunities and challenges, the experts give their opinion on the future of European logistics. In this section, the experts provide an outlook for logistics investments in Europe in the years to come. In particular, the following question is treated:

> **6a: Which markets would you consider the most attractive in the future for logistics investments and why?**

We have learned that the transport, traffic, and above all logistics will continue to be systemically important. This is becoming even more clear these days with a view of the geopolitical situation. The interruption and re-routing of transport flows will lead to a short-term increase in storage capacity. Which was already a lesson through the Covid-19 pandemic (Beyerle, 2022).

Catella's (2022a) forecast for the European logistics market (see Appendix B: Catella Logistics Market Map Europe 2022) shows that since their last published study in October 2021, prime rents for logistics have risen by an average of almost 3% across all 112 markets surveyed. Due to the sustained investor interest in the logistics segment, yield compression can be observed across all markets. The lowest net initial yields, in prime locations in Germany, as well as Paris and London, are hardly above 3%. It seems to be only a matter of time before the prime yield in the top locations falls below the 3% mark. In 2021 a record transaction volume of almost €60 billion was recorded at European level across the markets surveyed. This shows the increasing investor interest in logistics real estate in Europe. Nevertheless, the market for this asset class will find itself between further dynamic growth and increased risk provisioning on the part of investors in the coming months. CRBE (2022, pp. 12–15) also predicts that there will be ongoing disruptions and a surge in costs when it comes to the supply chain. There the focus will still be on supply chain priorities in the post-Covid-19 era. In particular, inventory control, meaning from just-in-time to just-in-case principles and the movement to closer consumption points, as well as diversifying sourcing and production bases to expand network resilience and agility.

Similarly, expectations of rental growth, low-interest rates, and strong investor demand are forecast to push yields lower. E-commerce-dedicated logistics space accounted for an estimated 20% of total European take-up in 2021. An increase in e-commerce and supply chain reconfiguration should continue to boost demand for logistics space over the medium term. In combination with constrained supply, this is forecast to continue to push up prime rents (Karmann, 2022).

Overall, it is tricky to give a market outlook for such a dynamic industry. Moreover, the future of European logistics is strongly dependent on the further course of the Russia-Ukraine war and the geopolitical situation globally. Despite the uncertainties, the experts reveal which markets in Europe they consider attractive for future logistics investments. What is being discussed in advance, however, is why these markets have a positive outlook and are therefore, considered attractive for investors. Essentially, a market is considered "attractive" when it fulfills the criteria of a *hub* in logistics. So, what distinguishes a *hub* in logistics? A hub must have a strong industrial- (mainly manufacturing and transportation) and infrastructure base, as well as a high population with a strong consumption and labor force (Steves, 2022).

According to these criteria, the four major logistics hubs in Europe are France, Germany, the Netherlands, and the UK (Karmann, 2022). Within Europe, the experts have named further submarkets that they consider attractive for future logistics investments. The markets that have often been mentioned are listed below (the locations have not been weighted by times mentioned nor are they in any specific order):

- Germany: Berlin, Hamburg, Munich, Nuremberg
- France: Paris, Marseille
- UK: London
- Netherlands: Amsterdam, Rotterdam
- Nordics: Finland, Sweden, Norway
- Spain: Barcelona, Madrid
- Italy: Milan, Rome, Bologna
- Austria: Vienna, Lienz
- Switzerland: Nyon
- Others: Hungary, Poland, Czech Republic

Logistics will continue to be a dynamic growth market. Therefore, each market must be considered individually when investing in logistics. But no matter in which market one invests in, Catella's (2022a) study shows that there is one warning signal that counts for all markets: The first risk premiums from financiers for project developments in this segment and the basic risk adjustment to the political-economic situation will put the multipliers or returns under pressure. In combination with constrained supply, this is forecast to continue to push up prime rents. Moreover, with the Russia-Ukraine war and the Fed's tightening of monetary policy, investors are increasingly focused on inflation and slowing economic growth (MSCI, 2022). Nevertheless, the experts agree that the outlook for the European logistics market, despite the fog, looks positive overall.

4.4 Interim Summary – Future of European Logistics

The future of the European logistics sector has been analyzed in this chapter. This subchapter gives a brief interim summary of the second part of the analysis: Experts on the Future of European Logistics.

ESG has risen quite high on the agenda of many investors and therefore, is a trend to watch out for when it comes to the future of European logistics. The recent pandemic has sharpened the ESG debate, as we have observed how nature thrived during the lockdowns and reduced production has led to notably lower emissions in most major global cities. The growth in ESG-focused funds will most likely lead to increased pressure and eventually material discounts on any company not keeping up.

The European logistics sector not only showed resilience during the strict lockdowns during H1 2020 but went on to benefit from consumer and business reactions to the pandemic during H2 2020. The experts' opinions on the market outlook broadly match the Cushman & Wakefields (2021, p. 15) logistics outlook. Namely that e-commerce, both geographically and by product range, will be a key driver of new space demand over the next decade. In a post-Covid-19 world, there will be a greater focus on using logistics real estate to leverage cost across the whole supply chain, and better positioning by reshoring, inventory management, labor issues, transportation, and ESG. Moreover, the future of European logistics is strongly dependent on the further course of the Russia-Ukraine war and the geopolitical situation globally. The strength of structural drivers promises to fuel demand for logistics space in Europe for the foreseeable future. Therefore, it is no surprise that investor pricing which has narrowed the spread between industrial and office yields, points to a consequential rise in logistics land values, therein implying faster-growing rents. It remains to be seen how the industry will react and where these higher rents will and will not be sustained (Cushman & Wakefield, 2021, p. 15).

In summary, although there are a lot of opportunities in investing in European logistics real estate, there are still some key issues to face. One of them being that logistics will continue to be a dynamic growth market. Therefore, each market must be considered individually when investing in logistics. Additionally, the first risk premiums from financiers for project developments in this segment and the basic risk adjustment to the political-economic situation will put the multipliers or returns under pressure. In combination with constrained supply, this is expected to continue to push up prime rents. Moreover, with the Russia-Ukraine war and the Fed's tightening of monetary policy, the focus is increasingly on inflation and slowing economic growth. A lot of discipline will be required in the future since investors are under great pressure to deploy money and generate return. Thus, investing in the right assets in this highly competitive market is arguably the biggest challenge for investors.

5 Investment Guide

Logistics properties in Europe are increasingly becoming the focus of real estate investors. Continued strong interest from investors is expected as the Covid-19 pandemic as well as economic and political instabilities underscore the important role of logistics and the robustness of this asset class. Based on the previous analyses, this chapter intends to provide investors with a guide for investments in European logistics. To do so, the experts answer the following final two questions:

7a: What will you look at when you develop or acquire an asset and why?

7b: Which recommendations are derivable for investors and how can they be implemented in terms of risk/return optimization?

5.1 Investment Criteria

First, the experts reveal what they will pay attention to when developing or acquiring an asset and why. Here too, the experts broadly agree on the investment criteria in European logistics. The upcoming sections highlight and explain some of the investment criteria. The reader will then find an overview of the mentioned assessment criteria for European logistics at the end of this subchapter (Figure 9: Overview Investment Criteria – European Logistics Real Estate).

The most obvious criterion is the location of the asset. The macro- and micro-location play an important role in the requirements. Regarding macro-location the property should be in a logistics region or conurbation, in proximity to a production site, and have optimal transport connection (railway, waterway, airway, highway). Ideal micro-location characteristics are, e.g., good infrastructure nearby and on-site, and no residential area in

T. T. Quach et al., *Logistics Real Estate*, https://doi.org/10.1007/978-3-658-42837-2_5

the neighborhood. Although picking and choosing favorite locations in a world where there is not enough space, will be quite hard. For this reason, Thomas Beyerle (2022) explains that Catella will focus on setting on existing transport corridors or clusters and develop things further from there. Basically, they settle at places where there is already much around or in areas where others potentially will settle around them in the future. The agglomeration principle is important to Catella and they avoid buying standalone properties.

Just as important as the location, is immediate access to major consumption centers, i.e., access to the gateways of global trade and economic networks. Metropolitan areas like London, Paris, Milan, and Berlin perform well because they are close to major population centers with high consumption and support an efficient supply chain (Prologis, 2017, p. 2).

Thomas Karmann (2022) explains that when it comes to value creation in the future, the legal environment of an area plays a key role as well. Therefore, AXA IM will attach great importance to geographical diversification in terms of the legal environment of the individual countries. A legal environment that allows to increase rent and adapt lease contracts over time is clearly preferred. Besides, since the European logistics market is quite competitive currently, AXA IM is adapting capital raising to their products where they currently can deploy capital easier and faster.

Moreover, the efficiency of the asset from a cargo flow point of view is important, or in other words the automation. Swiss Life AM Nordics raises the following additional questions when acquiring a logistics property: Who is the tenant? How good is the tenant in terms of profitability operation? (Because if the tenant is not profitable, the rents are not going to be paid.) Is the asset suitable for one or more tenants (Pedersen, 2022)?

Overall, the investment criteria are not much different from the criteria for other property asset classes (Pedersen, 2022). But when it comes to logistic buildings, infrastructure plays a main role, especially in the transport sector. Carla Seidel (2022) underlines again that ideally there should be more than one infrastructure connection (railway, waterway, airway, highway) around the property, and preferably the property should be in an urban area (not on a green field, because the duplication risk is higher). Furthermore, Swiss Life

Asset Managers looks at places that are growing demographically and economically. Additionally, with changing demographics and increased levels of value-added services in logistics facilities, the availability of qualified staff has become a structural as well as a cyclical driver in location selection. Therefore, BEOS Logistics must have clear answers to the labor force situation in the area, on how "constraint" the market is, i.e., know the hurdles. Moreover, ESG must of course be considered before acquiring or developing an asset (Steves, 2022).

Criterion	Description
Location	• The location is considered the most important criterion, as the location is not changeable once you have settled there. • No compromise on macro- & micro-location: Logistics conurbation, in proximity to a production site, optimal transport connection (road, wail, water, air), good infrastructure nearby and on-site, no residential area in the neighborhood
Purchase Price & Yield	The pruchase price and yield are important numbers with regard to risk/return optimization as you want your investment to be profitable.
Legal Environment	• The legal enviroment should allow the indexation of the lease structures to adapt your cash flow/rent growth. • Flexibility is key for value creation in the future.
Geographical Diversification	Diversifiaction is essential when it comes to investments. Minimize risks by geographical diversification of the assets.
Asset Itself	• Avoid duplication risk. • No compromise on generic & flexible asset characteristics: The automation degree is an important criterion in terms of efficiency of an assset.
ESG	• ESG is a key factor in every asset nowadays and ESG certifications get more and more important. • ESG is considered an image factor for a possible resale in the future.
Tenant	• Proper due diligence of the tenant is crucial: Who is the tenant? How profitable is the business? Are the employees happy? • It is an important criterion with regard to the coordination of global tenant management.
Market	Evaluation of everything connected to the market: demographics, purchase power, growth potential, submarkets, constraints, labour, etc.
Infrastructure	• The infrastructure plays a major role, especially in the transport sector. • Preferably the area has more than one infrastructure connections: railway, waterway, airway, highway.
Time	It is essential to consider time as a factor in terms of timing (time of purchase) and time horizon (length of the holding period).
Portfolio Size	A critical size of the portfolio is required to allow for active asset management.

Figure 9: **Overview Investment Criteria – European Logistics Real Estate**

5

Figure 9: Overview Investment Criteria – European Logistics Real Estate provides an outline of the expert's investment criteria for investments in European logistics.

5.2 Investment Principles

In this subchapter, the experts underline the key dimensions behind the potential and challenges of investments in logistics real estate by telling what investment principles are derivable for investors and how they can be implemented in terms of risk/return optimization. The principles are based on the current situation of European logistics (Chapter 3: Analysis I – Experts on the Current Situation of European Logistics) and the future dynamics which will shape European logistics (Chapter 4: Analysis II – Experts on the Future of European Logistics).

The upcoming sections highlight and explain some of the investment principles by the experts. The reader will then find an overview of the mentioned investment principles for European logistics at the end of this subchapter (Figure 10: Overview Investment Principles – European Logistics Real Estate). The guidelines of the experts do not differ greatly. The overall aim is to adhere to the following principles for a logistics investment in Europe to be successful in the long term in terms of risk/return optimization.

First of all, the investment criteria mentioned in the previous subchapter and listed in Figure 9: Overview Investment Criteria – European Logistics Real Estate should be considered for the assessment of a logistics investment property. On top of the assessment of the criteria list, the probably most important principle at the moment is: *Stay disciplined and patient.* Sounds simple but can be very tricky in a dynamic and competitive market – such as the European logistics market. As we have learned the European logistics market is attracting more and more investors due to several reasons, one of them being the attractive return on investment with limited risk. Due to the great popularity of this asset class, the current offer on the market is smaller than the demand. As a result, there are hardly any properties for sale and the ones for sale are enormously expensive. Hence, it has gotten more difficult to invest profitably in European logistics. Therefore, the best thing to do is not to rush to the market but rather to stay patient and disciplined. Rather look at your logistics investment as a "marathon" and not a "sprint". This way your investment in European logistics will allow you to be profitable in the long run (Pedersen, 2022; Steves, 2022).

Thorbjørn Pedersen (2022) further explains that the commodities prices are relatively high at the moment because of the ongoing Russia-Ukraine war. Russia and Ukraine have some valuable commodities that are needed all over the world. In that context, the war has an impact on the supply chain. In addition, investors have to take inflation and interest rate development into account. As a result, it is also taking longer for confidence to return and investment activity to pick up in Europe. European logistics as an asset class will find itself between further dynamic growth and increased risk provisioning in the coming months. There are a lot of uncertainties ahead of us which are not reflected in the asset prices, i.e., they have not come down (Haller, 2022; Hollung 2022). Therefore, another important recommendation is: *There is a lot of "fog" at the moment; do not invest like there is always "sunshine".*

No matter what the goal, the key to all investments is understanding your time horizon. When investing in European logistic properties, another piece of advice from the experts is: *Have a long-term look.* One of the most important criteria for investing is the time you give your investment to grow. Typically, long-term investing means five years or more, but there is no firm definition. However, a portfolio should give the investor predictability over five to ten years (Pedersen, 2022).

Diversification is a strategy that minimizes the risk to your portfolio by investing in a range of assets across several criteria. Logistics properties make a significant contribution to the diversification of a real estate portfolio, as logistics yields are driven by different factors from those of residential and office properties. Total returns on logistics premises exhibit a negative correlation with the residential properties and have virtually no correlation with office properties at all. Though, Bodo Hollung (2022) emphasizes that it is just as important to diversify within the asset class through the following points: location (geographical), type of property, users (trade, transport, production, contact logistics, etc.), tenant mix (large, mid-size, small), lease term/structures, and banks/refinancing (max. 3–4 properties with one bank). Another way to diversify the portfolio is to add value to existing assets, e.g., adding industrial properties to diversify the risks (Pfeiffer, 2022). Furthermore, a portfolio should have a critical size to allow for active asset management (Karmann, 2022). A good diversification strategy will ensure you receive stable returns. Thus, another key principle from the experts is: *Diversify.*

Finally, investing in logistics requires specific know-how that not every investor has in full. Here logistics platforms come in handy. Logistics platforms function as a partner who acquire and develop logistics real estate that match the investor's needs. They interact as the point of contact for investors throughout the whole value chain. BEOS Logistics (2022) is an example of such a logistics platform. BEOS Logistics develops high-quality logistics real estate and distribution centers in Europe. They create added value for all parties involved, acting as a reliable partner both to the companies that use the properties and to the cities and communities in which they are located. As an investor and property developer, BEOS Logistics plays a part in upholding the proper function of systemically important logistics infrastructure while guiding it on the path toward a sustainable future. Hence, the last principle is: *Have the right partner.*

Assess the Investment Criteria	See Figure 9: Overview Investment Criteria – European Logistics Real Estate.
Be Disciplined & Patient	The best thing to do in a dynamic and competitive market – such as the European logistics market – is to stay patient and disciplined. Do not rush things. This will allow your logistics investment to be profitable in the long-run.
Distinguish "Sunshine" / "Fog"	Economical and political uncertainties make it difficult to predict a market outlook for the European logistics market. Do not invest like there will always be "sunshine". Consider "fog" when investing, i.e., the uncertainties should be reflected in the asset price.
Have a Long-Term Look	To give your logistics investment time to grow, it is advisable to have a long-term investment horizon (> 5 years).
Diversify	A well diversified portfolio minimizes risk and gives stable returns. For logistics investments, it is advisable to invest in a range of assets across different locations, type of properties, users, tenants, lease terms/structures, and banks/refinancing.
Partner-Up	Logistics platform come in handy when specific logistics know-how is required. Having the right partner can help matching your needs more precisely.

Figure 10: **Overview Investment Principles - European Logistics Real Estate**

Figure 10: Overview Investment Principles – European Logistics Real Estate provides an outline of the expert's principles for investments in European logistics.

5.3 Investment Pitfalls

Despite the potential of the European logistics market, one must not overlook the fact that European logistics as an asset class comes with its own set of challenges. These should definitely be considered before investing. As the final part of the investment guide, this subchapter aims to underline the key pitfalls behind investments in European logistics. The reader will find an overview of the discussed investment pitfalls at the end of this chapter (Figure 11: Overview Investment Pitfalls – European Logistics Real Estate).

First and foremost, it is important for investors to know what exactly they are dealing with when talking about logistics. As logistics is very broadly defined, it is essential to specify what kind of building is of interest (see Figure 3: Logistics Real Estate – The 4 Sub-Asset Classes). The second thing to note is that logistics real estate cannot be treated in the same exact way as other real estate asset classes. Because of the fact that logistics properties are much more heterogeneous and specific than office and residential properties. This is one of the reasons why they are traded with a risk premium. Similarly, the smaller user base, consisting of industrial companies, retailers, and logistics service providers, leads to a more limited third-party usability (CBRE, 2020, p. 4).

Moreover, logistics will continue to be a dynamic growth market. Therefore, each market must be considered individually when investing in logistics. Plus, logistics is still a human capital-intensive business. Lots of people are typically required to operate within logistics buildings. However, there are long-standing and significant challenges around the recruitment of appropriate staff, particularly in skilled jobs. In result, investors should be aware that occupiers may not always be able to find the right labor. This could jeopardize their business, which in turn has a knock-on effect on the rent being paid late or not at all. Therefore, investors should not only focus on macro- and micro location, but also pay attention to the interior of the building to ensure staff attraction and retention, as well as performance (e.g., the inclusion of wellness and welfare space for workers and improved quality of the facilities overall) (Bruer, 2021; Karmann, 2022).

Also, land prices continue to rise in major urban areas, adding upwards pressure on capital values. Nevertheless, capital allocations towards the logistics sector remain strong because investors are willing to pay premiums to gain exposure to the sector and are now becoming less sensitive to location. Moreover, investors are now turning their attention to secondary assets to ride the yield wave. So, despite rising construction costs, speculative development in the sector is anticipated to rise during 2022/23 as investors move up the risk curve in search of higher returns (Savills, 2022, pp. 5–6). Accordingly, in this competitive market, investors should pay even more attention to the examination of individual assets, consider the risks, and not invest hastily just to participate in the "game" by ignoring the risks (Pedersen, 2022).

The Covid-19 pandemic has not yet been finally overcome and in addition, huge uncertainties come with the Russia-Ukraine war. Due to the Russia-Ukraine war the transport routes through Russia are interrupted which is probably the most incisive development in the logistics sector. Therefore, the development of European logistics investments is strongly dependent on the further course of the Russia-Ukraine war and the geopolitical situation globally. As a consequence, it is also taking longer for confidence to return and investment activity to pick up in Europe (Hollung, 2022). These uncertainties should be evaluated when investing. Catella's (2022a) study even shows that the first risk premiums from financiers for project developments in this segment and the basic risk adjustment to the political-economic situation will put the multipliers or returns under pressure. Furthermore, investors have to take interest rate development into account. With the Fed's tightening of monetary policy, investors should increasingly be alerted regarding inflation and slowing economic growth (MSCI, 2022).

Figure 11: Overview Investment Pitfalls – European Logistics Real Estate provides an outline of the key pitfalls investors should consider when investing in European logistics.

Heterogeneous Asset Class & Smaller User Base	Logistics properties are much more heterogeneous and specific than office and residential properties. They have a smaller user base and a more limited third-party usability which have to be considered.
Individual Markets	It is important to note that the evolvement of European logistics cannot simply be attributed to specific factors because the logistics market is a highly dynamic growth market. Therefore, each market must be assessed individually when investing in logistics.
Challenges Around the Workforce in Logistics	Long-standing and significant challenges around the recruitment of appropriate staff in the logistics sector must be considered. If this results in the tenant's business not running, delays or loss of rent can occur for the investor.
Rising Land Prices & Speculative Investments	Rising land prices in major urban areas are adding upward pressure on capital values. Investors venture into speculative investment to participate in higher returns. Careful assessment of the investment criteria thus becomes even more important (see Figure 9: Overview Investment Criteria - European Logistics Real Estate).
Geopolitical Uncertainties	The development of European logistics is strongly dependent on the further course of the Russia-Ukraine war and the geopolitical situation globally. As a result, it takes longer for confidence to return and investment activity to pick up plus risk adjustments will put returns under pressure.
Further Alerts	With the Fed's tightening of monetary policy, investors should be alerted regarding inflation and slowing economic growth.

Figure 11: **Overview Investment Pitfalls - European Logistics Real Estate**

6 Conclusion

In the conclusion, the defined research questions RQ1-RQ6 (see Chapter 1.1: Research Aim & Questions) are answered. Moreover, a critical reflection of this research paper and a suggestion for further research in this field are given.

6

6.1 Answers to Research Questions

RQ1: What is the current situation in the European logistics market?

The Covid-19 crisis highlighted the key role played by logistics. European logistics has proved to be dynamic and crisis resistant. The current situation is characterized by the following:

- Surplus in demand with constrained supply in logistics spaces
- Low vacancy rates
- Trends like deglobalization, e-commerce, and last link logistics boost the demand
- Covid-19 accelerated the e-commerce trend
- Higher demand for logistics space in urban areas
- Shift in supply chains (supply chain resilience – safety inventory, onshoring/nearshoring)
- Uncertainties due to political and economic instability globally
- Need for more flexibility and agility (automation)
- Overall, a positive market assessment

So, demographic, economic, and technological trends, as well as political risks, are currently driving the European logistics market. The surplus in demand and the shortage of logistics spaces are reflected in the low vacancy rates. An increase in e-commerce and supply chain reconfiguration is

T. T. Quach et al., *Logistics Real Estate*, https://doi.org/10.1007/978-3-658-42837-2_6

boosting demand even further, especially in urban areas. Nevertheless, with the Russia-Ukraine war and the uncertainties that come with it, new requirements in terms of flexibility and agility have arisen for the logistics sector. Overall, the European logistics market remains a growing industry.

RQ2: What are the current megatrends that are shaping European logistics?

The past years have accelerated and highlighted some existing trends but have also shown new emerging trends. The key megatrends that are currently shaping the European logistics sector are:

- Deglobalization & Supply Chains Resilience
- E-Commerce Penetration
- Last Link Logistics
- Automatization & Electrification

The trend of deglobalization and onshoring/nearshoring has a significant impact on the European logistics sector. The geopolitical situation has become an increasingly important driver, especially when it comes to supply chains. Moreover, increasing attention to the environmental impact of supply chains is leading to regionalization and optimization of goods flows. As a result, companies, and stakeholders are increasingly focused on supply chain resilience.

Since the onset of the pandemic, online retail sales have surged across all major European economies. The increase in e-commerce is boosting demand for additional logistics spaces. Furthermore, last link logistics thrive on the e-commerce trend. The problem is that there is rarely space available and construction in urban areas has proven difficult. However, last link logistics is also influenced by the end consumers since a parcel can be brought and picked up by consumers themselves.

Logistics is a labor-intensive business. The high cost of labor and the relatively low cost of capital lead to the trend of automation. A growing shortage of skilled labor, an explosion in demand from occupiers, and some intriguing technological advances fuel this trend even to a greater extent. In addition, electrification of vehicles is an important trend in the European logistics sector; with good reason because transport accounts for more than 16% of greenhouse gas emissions globally and 25% of GHG emissions in the EU. In the pressure to decarbonize logistics, cooperations and alliances are taking off to tackle the decarbonization challenge.

RQ3: How does the European logistics market currently look like regarding investments?

The market for European logistics investments is currently characterized by the following:

- High investors' interest and high competition
- Yield compression
- Rising prime rents
- High transaction volumes
- Low vacancy

Due to the sustained investor interest in the logistics segment, yield compression and rising rental prices can be observed across all markets in Europe. The current European average yield is at an average of 4.68%. The lowest net initial yields can be found in prime locations, e.g., Germany and the Netherlands (3–3.40%). In addition, prime rents for logistics have gone up to €16.40/m^2 for prime logistics spaces. The current strong demand for logistics properties can also be seen in the record transaction volumes which go up to almost €20 billion in the UK. In total, an investment volume of around €60 billion was recorded across 112 countries in Europe, which also represents a new record transaction volume at the European level.

Expectations of rental growth, low-interest rates, and strong investor demand coupled with continued low vacancy are forecast to push yields even lower. In addition, the sustained investor interest in the asset class is being met by a changed geopolitical situation in Europe. However, capital allocations towards the logistics sector remain strong, and despite rising construction costs, speculative development in the sector is anticipated to rise during 2022/23 as investors move up the risk curve in search of higher returns. Therefore, it is also anticipated that there is still further room for yields to move in for the best stock, particularly in non-core locations. Overall,

European logistics is expected to remain of considerable interest to investors mainly due to the following attributes of this asset class:

- Stable cash flows
- Low CapEx (Capital Expenditure)
- Simplicity/manageability
- High liquidity
- Tenants with good credit ratings
- Rental growth potential

RQ4: How will logistics take on ESG?

ESG has become a key factor in every asset class – consequentially, also in European logistics real estate. The transformation of the logistics markets is expected to be faster than in the office or residential market since the pressure on the logistics industry is greater. Especially, the EU taxonomy will put a lot of pressure on European logistics real estate.

Regarding the *environment* side, much of the sustainability features of buildings have been focused on how to reduce carbon emissions through the usage of the buildings. However, the biggest shift that will affect the industry, is the impact of how the industry deals with construction and maintaining the logistics buildings. These are some possible sustainable solutions:

- Electrifications of vehicles
- On-site renewables
- Efficient sealing of the surface
- Solar panels
- LED lighting
- Carbon-neutral constructions
- Using recycled materials
- Air- or groundwater heat pumps
- Biodiversity (increase the natural value of the land)

The growth in green energy has created new opportunities for landlords and currently attracts large subsidies from the EU. As a result, fitting logistics buildings with solar panels – either to sell to tenants or sell back to the grid – can be highly accretive to returns. Furthermore, the growth in green-oriented fund management is likely to see carbon-neutral logistics attract a decent premium in capital markets. Nevertheless, the main share of logistics' greenhouse gas emissions is from the emissions through the movement of goods by different modes of transport, noticeably from road freight. This means the greatest gains can be made by the mitigation or the reduction of greenhouse gas emissions through the transport side of the logistics industry.

Regarding the *social* side of ESG, warehouses typically rely on large pools of labor. New jobs can be created in the logistics sector by developing new large-format schemes in areas of high unemployment. There is a chance automation may limit this somewhat, although in the short-term it is likely that labor will still be important for most occupiers.

Regarding the *governance* side of ESG, topics like employee well-being and reasonable company management have shifted into focus. Securing employees for the logistics business is getting more and more important and therefore, the inclusion of wellness and welfare space for workers and improved quality of the facilities overall is crucial. It is about making sure that those occupiers have the tools in place for them to operate effectively and efficiently. With regard to tenant retention, this is not only an important criterion for occupiers but also investors. At the end of the day, the tenant and the employees need to be happy and healthy to stay in the building.

RQ5: What opportunities and challenges will drive the future of European logistics?

Regarding opportunities, the simplest and probably most valuable point is that logistics is basic infrastructure; it is not like a shopping mall or a fancy office building. Therefore, macroeconomic risks do not play a major role when it comes to investments in logistics. Furthermore, the experts predict e-commerce penetration to continue which will also represent a big opportunity for the logistics sector. Another opportunity is that many firms that are currently operating in old facilities are going to need new facilities sooner or later, because new facilities operate more economical. This in turn creates new investment opportunities. The old facilities can be renovated, or even demolished, and new logistics buildings can be created. Additional potential come with megatrends like last link logistics which is in high demand and

ESG where investors can add a green premium. From an investor's perspective, there are hardly any concerns when it comes to the fundamental drivers influencing the European logistics market.

However, when it comes to the challenges, supply is limited, and the lack of space availability is beside the resistance toward construction activities in the inner-city, a hurdle to handle. Another challenge is that this industry is hardly creating new jobs – which does not make the plausibility of a new logistics building in an urban area easier. Moreover, the transport routes through Russia are interrupted which is probably the most incisive development in the logistics sector. There is a possible risk that European logistics funds will suffer due to their investments in countries close to Russia (e.g., Poland, the Czech Republic, Slovenia, and Hungary). Furthermore, investors have to take inflation and interest rate development into account. As a result, it is also taking longer for confidence to return and investment activity to pick up in Europe. Concretely this means, this asset class will find itself between further dynamic growth and increased risk provisioning in the coming months. To master these challenges the industry must become more efficient through innovation, quickly adapt to change, and develop holistic thinking toward ESG. In particular, the optimization of transport routes must be a priority in the future. To boost this, the governments and authorities must be cooperative as well, i.e., have an open mind towards logistics. Only this way the excess demand in European logistics can be met in the future.

RQ6: What are recommendations for investors in terms of targeting regions, risk/return optimization, and how to implement future trends in an investment portfolio?

Essentially, a logistics market is considered a targeting region when it fulfills the criteria of a logistics *hub*. A hub must have a strong industrial- and infrastructure base, as well as a major population center with a strong consumption and labor force. Moreover, the attractiveness and connectivity of the place play a role. People want to work in places that are nice and that are easy for them to access. This is important for occupiers but also for investors, and developers in terms of tenant retention. Just as important, is immediate access to major consumption centers, i.e., access to the gateways of global trade and economic networks. Within Europe the following markets are considered targeting regions for future logistics investments because they are close to consumers and support an efficient supply chain:

- Germany: Berlin, Hamburg, Munich, Nuremberg
- France: Paris, Marseille
- UK: London
- Netherlands: Amsterdam, Rotterdam
- Nordics: Finland, Sweden, Norway
- Spain: Barcelona, Madrid
- Italy: Milan, Rome, Bologna
- Austria: Vienna, Lienz
- Switzerland: Nyon
- Others: Hungary, Poland, Czech Republic

In terms of returns, yield compression has been observed in all markets across Europe due to the sustained investor interest in this asset class. Expectations of rental growth, low-interest rates, and strong investor demand are forecast to push yields even lower. Prime rents for logistics have risen by an average of almost 3% compared to last year. The lowest net initial yields are hardly above 3% and can be found in prime locations in Germany, as well as Paris and London. It seems to be only a matter of time before the prime yield in the top locations falls below the 3% mark. However, logistics can continue to make a positive contribution to the overall return of a portfolio, even if the yield premium compared to other real estate asset classes is disappearing. Logistics properties make a significant contribution to the diversification of a real estate portfolio, as logistics yields are driven by different factors from those of residential and office properties. Total returns on logistics premises exhibit a negative correlation with the residential properties and have virtually no correlation with office properties at all. A combination of scarcity of supply and healthy long-term demand outlook makes logistics real estate attractive to investors. No structural reasons are pointing to any decline in demand in the future. In terms of risk, nevertheless, with the Russia-Ukraine war and the Fed's tightening of monetary policy, investors should be increasingly alerted regarding inflation and slowing economic growth.

In the coming years, the European logistics segment will benefit from megatrends such as e-commerce, new technologies, deglobalization, and more.

However, some investment criteria must be met to implement these future trends into a portfolio and hence, to profit from the long-term growth potential in the European logistics market. The implementation of new technologies, e.g., in logistics can complement and enhance human skills and productivity. They also make workplaces safer and more accurate. To profit from this trend investors need to invest in logistics facilities that work now and in the future. Moreover, Investors should rather settle in established logistics areas with demographic and economic growth potential rather than buy stand-alone properties. Additionally, the asset should have more than one infrastructure connection (railway, waterway, airway, highway). Furthermore, it is important to be in a legal environment that allows rent increases and lease contract adaptions over time to implement future trends and create value for the portfolio. Finally, since ESG and automation are clear trends to watch in the future, ESG criteria as well as the efficiency of the property have to be well assessed before acquiring or developing an asset.

6.2 Critical Reflection & Further Research

The following chapter is divided into critical reflection and recommendation for further research. In the first section, the integrated approach of this work is critically assessed. In the second section, a recommendation for further research is given based on the findings from this work.

Critical Reflection

Due to the limited research period and scope of this research, the topic had to be narrowed down. Since the topic of *European Logistics* is very extensive, the matter has been treated rather superficially and in the sense of an overview, rather than going into detail. This also corresponds to the aim of this work, namely, to present the fundamentals of logistics investments and their assessment criteria, so readers can orientate themselves within the European logistics market.

First and foremost, this work represents a guideline based on academic research and is not a specific investment recommendation. Nonetheless, this guide must be critically scrutinized. The research of European logistics mainly revolves around trends and market outlooks. Hereby, it is important to note that the evolvement of European logistics – or logistics in general, cannot simply be attributed to specific factors because the logistics market is a highly dynamic growth market. Any conclusions made on the future direction of the European logistics market should be considered with caution as unforeseen events or elements can still shape the development.

The current situation has been presented by considering the developments of the past few years, starting especially with the pandemic. Earlier developments, however, have most likely also affected the situation today. A more in-depth analysis should, therefore, be carried out to create a more complete picture of the European logistics sector.

This work uses a qualitative research approach. In detail, the qualitative approach perceives and analysis the data gathered from the literature review and from the interviews through an academic lens. The contributors to this work, i.e., the experts interviewed, were asked to reflect on their own experiences and share their insights on European logistics. The experts have different starting points, and experiences, and therefore, the interviews can lead to differences in opinion. This book treats all experts' opinions neutrally and weighted them the same. The experts' answers to the interview questions were simply compared with each other to identify similarities or differences. Besides, the answers were compared to the literature review. Other than that, the answers were not further questioned, i.e., the experts' answers were not critically reflected on whether they have true value. The presented work is the result of broad first-hand contributions (interviews), careful secondary research, and a thorough analysis of said research. However, working with expert contribution and secondary research also means trusting the opinions and work of others. Naturally, the sources were checked for their reputation within the market.

Another critical point is that only experts from this field were interviewed. Experts from this field usually want to support their field of expertise and present it as positively as possible. This can lead to insights based on the interpretation of a subjective matter. No "critical" opinions were obtained, i.e., no "opponents" of the logistics industry were interviewed. This implies that the work tends to be biased because only representatives of the logistics industry give their opinion and no comparison to non-supporter is presented.

Furthermore, the weakness of this work is that the expert opinions were not substantiated with numbers and facts, i.e., a quantitative approach is missing. Other ways of conducting research and thereby extending and enriching the knowledge base of European logistics, are e.g., using a quantitative approach or *mixed methods* design. By using both qualitative and quantitative methods within one study, the findings can provide a richer understanding and more robust explanations. Although using mixed methods in logistics research is rare, it can help to better understand the findings than with only a qualitative or quantitative, respectively.

In conclusion, there is still a need for the development of the methodological toolbox of this work to make this study more robust. The issues that were not addressed in this book will be found in the suggestions for further research.

Further Research

In general, there are a great number of publications on European logistics – even if, some of them include individual aspects, especially from fund providers. An overall view, with European logistics as the central focus, written from an economic point of view, is rarer. An overall view should include, in addition to the opinions of logistics advocates, critical voices against this asset class. This would strengthen the quality and reliability of the study. Of course, what would also increase the added value and power of a work, is an increased number of respondents, as well as more specific interview questions (e.g., broken down into the individual logistics markets). But unfortunately, that would have gone beyond the scope of this research.

This study gives an overview of logistics across Europe. It goes without saying that within Europe, every market is individual with its own dynamics. Therefore, every location should be analyzed on its own when making an investment decision. Another recommendation for further research, therefore, is to carry out the same study, with the same questions, on the individual countries or the major logistics cities/hubs across Europe. The country-specific guides would help investors to match their needs more precisely.

The issue of only using a qualitative approach in this work, highlights tools related to mixed methods which should help researchers provide a deeper and richer understanding of European logistics and at the same time deliver more profound findings. In general, logistics is a field continuously and constantly expanding, becoming more and more complex, and therefore needs a variety of methods to understand and explain it. Mixed method is mentioned as one, but a further factor for profound research is the time period. It would be exciting to see how European logistics will develop over a longer period of time – especially, in this "hectic" and "eventful" time in which we find ourselves nowadays. Collecting data over a longer time period would heighten the integrity of the work, therefore, suggested to other researchers in the field, especially to strengthen the validity of the conclusions given on future market developments.

Though, to depart from today's approach to logistics and supply chain problems, it requires rethinking basic assumptions of theories and paradigms such as structure, behavior, and relation to time. What also needs to be investigated, when it comes to the future of European logistics investments, are factors like speculation and greed from human character. Nevertheless, these factors are rather "utopian" and are probably better addressed within the framework of behavioral sciences.

Bibliography

AMAZON. (2021, February 03). *Amazon's custom electric delivery vehicles are starting to hit the road.* Retrieved April 10, 2022, from https://www.aboutamazon.com/news/transportation/amazons-custom-electric-delivery-vehicles-are-starting-to-hit-the-road

AO ARCHITECTS. (2022). *AO Architects.* Retrieved April 29, 2022, from https://www.aoarchitects.com/project/fulfillment-center/

AXA IM. (n.a.). *Environmental, social and governance.* Retrieved May 08, 2022, from https://www.axa-im.com/who-we-are/environmental-social-and-governance?msclkid=94d3ae26ced611ecba7d5c209a00d370

AXA INVESTMENT MANAGERS. (2021). *Immobilien in Europa: Wo gibt es Opportunitäten?* Retrieved November 09, 2021, from https://qualified.axa-im.ch/documents/25277/26689870/Pr%C3%A4sentation+Immobilien+Europa+20210428.pdf/f4f0466d-bcb2-4c71-5d34-211fee40e139?t=1619684342575

AXA INVESTMENT MANAGERS. (2022). *Genericlogisticsub-asset classes.*

BCG. (2021, July 29). *Real-World Supply Chain Resilience.* Retrieved May 29, 2022, from https://www.bcg.com/publications/2021/building-resilience-strategies-to-improve-supply-chain-resilience

BELL, E., BRYMAN, A., & HARLEY, B. (2018). *Business Research Methods* (5 ed.). Oxford University Press.

BELL, E., BRYMAN, A., & HARLEY, B. (2019). *Business Research Methods.* Oxford University Press.

BEOS LOGISTICS GMBH. (2022). *BEOS Logistics.* Retrieved April 20, 2022, from https://www.beos-logistics.net/

BEYERLE, T. (2022, April 04). Interview – European Logisitics. (T. Quach, Interviewer)

BIZ CHOICE. (2022). *Integrated Logistics Warehouse Program.* Retrieved April 29, 2022, from https://www.bizchoiceins.com/IntegratedLogisticsWarehouseProgram.aspx

BNP PARIBAS REAL ESTATE. (2021). *European Logistics Market.* Issy Les Moulineaux Cedex: BNP Paribas Real Estate. Retrieved November 02, 2021, from https://www.realestate.bnpparibas.com/#contact

BOGNER, A., LITTIG, B., & MENZ, W. (2014). *Interviews mit Experten: Eine praxisorientierte Einführung.* Wiesbaden: Springer Fachmedien.

T. T. Quach et al., *Logistics Real Estate*, https://doi.org/10.1007/978-3-658-42837-2

Bruer, S. (2021, May 04). Future of Logistic Real Estate. *Future of Logistic Real Estate Panel, May 2021.* Online Briefing: Real Asset Live TV. Retrieved 11 26, 2021, from https://realassetlive.com/media/future-of-logistic-real-estate-panel-may-2021/

Catella. (2021). *Der Markt für Logistikimmobilieninvestments in Europa – Renditechancen unter Risiken und Nebenwirkungen.* Retrieved December 24, 2021, from https://www.catella.com/globalassets/global/mix-germany-corporate-finance/catella_mt_logistik_black_swan_vi.pdf

Catella. (2021a). *Catella Infografik: Wertschöpfungsketten, Reshoring und Logistikmärkte.* Retrieved December 24, 2021, from https://www.catella.com/globalassets/global/mix-germany-corporate-finance/infografik_lieferketten_de.pdf

Catella. (2021c, July 15). *Catella Real Estate erwirbt rund 8.200m² großes light Industrialobjekt bei Freiburg für den Fonds „Catella Logistik Deutschland Plus".* Retrieved December 26, 2021, from https://www.catella.com/de/deutschland/neuigkeiten-und-pressemitteilungen/press-releases/2021/catella-real-estate-erwirbt-rund-8.200-m-grobes-light-industrialobjekt-bei-freiburg-fur-den-fonds-catella-logistik-deutschland-plus

Catella. (2022a, March 10). *Catella.* Retrieved May 12, 2022, from https://www.catella.com/en/germany/research/catella-logistics-market-map-europe-2022

Catella. (2022b). *European Logistics Markets 2022.* Retrieved May 08, 2022, from https://www.catella.com/globalassets/global/mix-germany-corporate-finance/catella_logistikkarte_2022.pdf

CBRE. (2020). *LOGISTICS REAL ESTATE REPORT SWITZERLAND 2020.* Retrieved December 26, 2021, from https://www.cbre.ch/-/media/cbre/countryswitzerland/documents/research/major-reports/logistics-real-estate-report-switzerland-2020.pdf

CBRE. (2021). *Switzerland – Logistics and Light Industrial Real Estate.* Retrieved December 24, 2021, from https://www.cbre.ch/-/media/cbre/countryswitzerland/Documents/Research/Major-Reports/Logistics_and_Light_Industrial_Real_Estate_Switzerland_2021.pdf

CBRE. (2022). *Global Industrial & Logistics Outlook.*

Corpus Sireo. (2021, February 02). *Swiss Life Asset Managers und BEOS erwerben Bremer Logistikimmobilie für europäischen Industrie- und LogistikFonds.* Retrieved May 30, 2022, from https://www.corpussireo.com/de-de/presse/pressemitteilungen/presspages/2021/2021-02-02-swiss-life-asset-managers-und-beos-erwerben

Credit Suisse. (2021a). *Home Sweet Home – Swiss Real Estate Market 2021.* Retrieved May 10, 2022, from https://www.credit-suisse.com/media/assets/private-banking/docs/ch/privatkunden/eigenheim-finanzieren/cs-immobilienstudie-2021-en.pdf

Credit Suisse. (2021b). *Real estate – Exploiting structural trends in real estate.* Retrieved December 25, 2021, from https://www.credit-suisse.com/microsites/investment-outlook/en/main-asset-classes/real-estate.html

Credit Suisse Asset Management. (2018). *Logistics Real Estate Report 2018.* Retrieved December 26, 2021, from https://www.credit-suisse.com/pwp/am/downloads/marketing/br_ch0245633950_ch_en_web.pdf

Cushman & Wakefield. (2018, September 20). *5 future drivers for retail and logistics.* Retrieved March 19, 2022, from https://cushmanwakefield.com.ua/en/5-future-drivers-retail-and-logistics

Cushman & Wakefield. (2019). *Last Link.* Retrieved 11 27, 2021, from https://www.cushmanwakefield.com.ua/sites/default/files/2020-02/CUS42002904%20Last%20Link%20Report_v13.pdf

Cushman & Wakefield. (2019). *Last Link.* Retrieved November 27, 2021, from https://www.cushmanwakefield.com.ua/sites/default/files/2020-02/CUS42002904%20Last%20Link%20Report_v13.pdf

Cushman & Wakefield. (2019). *Logistics Outlook 2020.*

Cushman & Wakefield. (2021, May 17). *Global Logistics Outlook.* Retrieved April 12, 2022, from https://cw-gbl-gws-prod.azureedge.net/-/media/cw/global/insights/global-outlook-logistics/2021-global-logistics-outlook.pdf?la=en&rev=b381a73a8ac04b88bd1cdeed6165e527&hash=BF3A4B0CE276CCC393547C772A9A4EF8

DIWG. (2021). *Logistics Properties.* Retrieved December 24, 2021, from https://www.diwg.de/wp-content/uploads/2021/10/2021_Trendreport_Logistik_FINAL.pdf

Exporo. (n.d.). *Immobilien Investment.* Retrieved April 30, 2021, from https://exporo.de/immobilien-investment/

Flick, U. (2018). *An Introduction to Qualitative Research* (Vol. 6). SAGE Publications.

Galletta, A. (2013). *Mastering the Semi-Structured Interview and Beyond: From Research Design to Analysis and Publication.* New York: New York University Press.

Guest, G., MacQueen, K. M., & Namey, E. E. (2012). *Introduction to applied thematic analysis.* Thousand Oaks, CA: SAGE Publications, Inc.

Gütle, T. (2021). *Perspectives on European Logistics and Light Industrial.* Primera Advisors GmbH.

Haller, M. (2021). *Logistics in Switzerland / Case Study Gateway Basel Nord.* Gateway Basel Nord.

Haller, M. (2022, March 24). Interview – European Logisitics. (T. Quach, Interviewer)

Hollung, B. (2022, March 10). Interview – European Logistics. (T. Quach, Interviewer)

JLL. (2020, July 09). *Industrial real estate demand to grow to 1 billion square feet by 2025.* Retrieved March 19, 2022, from https://www.us.jll.com/en/newsroom/industrial-real-estate-demand-to-grow-to-1b-sf-by-2025

JLL. (2021, March 05). *Logistik – Ein Immobiliensegment auf der Überholspur.* Retrieved November 07, 2021, from https://www.jll.ch/de/trends-and-insights/investoren/logistik-auf-der-ueberholspur

JLL. (2022). *European Logistics Market Update.* Retrieved April 11, 2022, from https://www.jll.de/en/trends-and-insights/research/european-logistics-market-update-february-2022

Karmann, T. (2022, February 24). Interview – European Logisitics. (T. T. Quach, Interviewer)

Kvale, S. (1996). *InterViews: An Introduction to Qualitative Research Interviewing.* Thousand Oaks, CA: SAGE Publications.

McKinsey & Company. (2019, April 24). *Automation in logistics: Big opportunity, bigger uncertainty.* Retrieved April 10, 2022, from https://www.mckinsey.com/industries/travel-logistics-and-infrastructure/our-insights/automation-in-logistics-big-opportunity-bigger-uncertainty

McKinsey & Company. (2021, April 30). *Succeeding in the AI supply-chain revolution.* Retrieved November 2, 2021, from https://www.mckinsey.com/industries/metals-and-mining/our-insights/succeeding-in-the-ai-supply-chain-revolution

Metapack. (2022). *Metapack.* Retrieved April 29, 2022, from https://www.metapack.com/de/solutions/letzte-meile-logistik/?utm_source=bing&utm_medium=ppc&utm_campaign=last+mile+delivery&msclkid=59a0423740371634f2fb205cf81a4b7c

MSCI. (2022, April 04). *Fed Policy and the Threat of Stagflation.* Retrieved April 10, 2022, from https://www.msci.com/www/blog-posts/fed-policy-and-the-threat-of/03104293171?utm_source=onemsci&utm_medium=email&utm_campaign=msci-weekly-2022-04-07

Pedersen, T. (2022, April 05). Interview – European Logistics. (T. Quach, Interviewer)

Pfeiffer, B. (2022, April 06). Interview – European Logisitics. (T. Quach, Interviewer)

Prologis. (2017). *CUSTOMER GROWTH STRATEGIES: EUROPE'S MOST DESIRABLE LOGISTICS LOCATIONS.* Retrieved March 15, 2022, from https://www.prologis.com/sites/corporate/files/documents/2017/10/prologis-research_europes-most-desirable-logistics-locations.pdf

Prologis. (2021). *Forever Altered: The Future of Logistics Real Estate Demand.* Retrieved December 25, 2021, from https://prologis.getbynder.com/m/25ce45ad24c53689/original/The-Future-of-Logistics-Real-Estate-Demand.pdf

Prologis. (n.d.). *GLOBAL SUPPLY CHAIN MANAGEMENT.* Retrieved December 26, 2021, from https://www.prologis.com/global-supply-chain-management

pwc. (2021). *Transport & Logistics Barometer.* Retrieved December 24, 2021, from https://www.pwc.de/de/transport-und-logistik/pwc-transport-and-logistics-barometer-h1-2021.pdf

pwc. (2022). *Transport & Logistics Barometer.* Retrieved April 10, 2022, from https://www.pwc.de/de/transport-und-logistik/transport-and-logistics-barometer/pwc-transport-and-logistics-barometer-h2-2021.pdf

Savills. (2021). *European Logistics Outlook.* Retrieved May 22, 2022, from https://pdf.euro.savills.co.uk/european/european-investments/european-logistics-outlook-sept-2021.pdf

Savills. (2022). *European Logistics Outlook.* Retrieved May 22, 2022, from https://pdf.euro.savills.co.uk/european/european-investments/spotlight---european-logistics-outlook-february-2022-.pdf

SEIDEL, C. (2022, March 23). Interview – European Logistics. (T. Quach, Interviewer)

STEVES, I. (2022, April 01). Interview – European Logistics. (T. Quach, Interviewer)

SUPPLY CHAIN DIGITAL. (2020, May 17). *Supply Chain Digital Europe's largest parcel hub completed for DPD.* Retrieved April 29, 2022, from https://supplychaindigital.com/logistics/europes-largest-parcel-hub-completed-dpd

SWISS LIFE ASSET MANAGERS. (2020a). *Benefiting from structural shifts in the economic landscape: European Industrial & Logistics.* Retrieved November 07, 2021, from https://www.swisslife-am.com/content/dam/slam/documents_publications/real-estate-research-reports/SLAM%20Research_EIL%20Report_Industrial%20and%20Logsitics_EN.pdf

SWISS LIFE ASSET MANAGERS. (2020b, September 11). *Anlagestiftung Swiss Life setzt Wachstumskurs fort und lanciert in Zusammenarbeit mit Swiss Life Asset Managers eine neue Anlagelösung für europäische Industrie- & Logistik-Immobilien.* Retrieved November 09, 2021, from https://www.swisslife-am.com/de/home/media/news/switzerland/institutional/2020/20200911_swiss_life_am_industrial_and_logistics_launch.html

SWISS LIFE ASSET MANAGERS. (2020b). *Anlagestiftung Swiss Life setzt Wachstumskurs fort und lanciert in Zusammenarbeit mit Swiss Life Asset Managers eine neue Anlagelösung für europäische Industrie- & Logistik-Immobilien.* Retrieved November 09, 2021, from https://www.swisslife-am.com/de/home/media/news/switzerland/institutional/2020/20200911_swiss_life_am_industrial_and_logistics_launch.html

SWISS LIFE ASSET MANAGERS. (2020c, December 09). *Successful launch of the new investment solution for European industrial and logistics and acquisition of three high-quality properties.* Retrieved December 24, 2021, from https://www.swisslife-am.com/en/home/media/news/switzerland/institutional/2020/20201209_erfolgreiche_lancierung_eil.html

SWISS LIFE ASSET MANAGERS. (2021, August 24). *Swiss Life Asset Managers erweitert ihr Portfolio mit dem Erwerb von Toplogistikobjekten in ganz Europa.* Retrieved December 24, 2021, from https://www.swisslife-am.com/de/home/media/news/corporate/company-news/2021/20210824_acquisition_logistic.html

SWISS LIFE ASSET MANAGERS. (2022, January 20). *Swiss Life Asset Managers erwirbt Logistikimmobilie in den Niederlanden.* Retrieved May 11, 2022, from https://ch.swisslife-am.com/de/home/media/news/germany/institutional/swiss-life-asset-managers-erwirbt-logistikimmobilie-in-den-niederlanden.html?msclkid=d2ec7f67d16011ecb7633b973d3af445

TOLLIVER, J., GRAHAM, L., & BROWN, D. (2021). *Global Logistics Outlook.* Cushman & Wakefield. Retrieved December 24, 2021, from https://cw-gbl-gws-prod.azureedge.net/-/media/cw/global/insights/global-outlook-logistics/2021-global-logistics-outlook_final.pdf?rev=e82964f10b86418298179c7ec705f17f

UBS ASSET MANAGEMENT. (2020). *Logistics post-COVID.* Retrieved December 25, 2021, from https://www.ubs.com/content/dam/assets/am/global/insights/asset-class-research/real-assets/real-estate-global/doc/white-paper-logistics-post-covid.pdf

VECTOR. (2021, March 23). *Just in Time (JIT) Logistics, Explained in Detail.* Retrieved December 25, 2021, from: https://www.withvector.com/blog/just-in-time-jit-logistics-explained-in-detail

WIKIPEDIA. (2021, November 26). *White-label product.* Retrieved April 10, 2022, from https://en.wikipedia.org/wiki/White-label_product#:~:text=A%20white-label%20product%20is%20a%20product%20or%20service,filled%20in%20with%20the%20marketer%27s%20trade%20dress%20.

WIKIPEDIA. (2022a, April 05). *EU taxonomy for sustainable activities.* Retrieved April 05, 2022, from: https://en.wikipedia.org/wiki/EU_taxonomy_for_sustainable_activities

WIKIPEDIA. (2022b, March 25). *BREEAM.* Retrieved May 11, 2022, from https://en.wikipedia.org/wiki/BREEAM?msclkid=c5b93adcd16b11ec82dd2cdd1f193dcf

WORLD TRADE ORGANIZATION. (2021). *World trade and economic growth 2020–21.* Retrieved December 26, 2021, from https://www.wto.org/english/res_e/statis_e/wts2021_e/wts2021chapter03_e.pdf

Appendices

T. T. Quach et al., *Logistics Real Estate*, https://doi.org/10.1007/978-3-658-42837-2

Appendix A: Evaluation Grid

		Similarities	Differences
1	**Overview**		
a	How do you assess the current situation in the European logistics sector?	• Charaterized by strong competition: Surplus in demand for logistics properties and shortage of space • Users are asking for more space for storage (safety function), especially in cities or peri-urban areas. • More foreign investors want to participate in the European logistics market. • New requirements for the logistics sector have arisen. • Covid-19 exhalerated the demand in this asset class. Trends like e-commerce and re-shoring, as well as the strong economic growth the past years have boosted this asset class even more.	**Thomas Beyerle:** On the one hand a boom market, on the other hand risky because of the political and economical instabilities which lead to uncertainty about the supply chain. However, overall, a positive view of the market.
2	**Megatrends**		
a	What changes do you see in terms of deglobaliza-tion, supply chain or e-commerce?	• The coronavirus highlighted the key role of logistics and the relative resilience of the sector, i.e., sparked the discussions about deglobalization. • The geo-political situation is a major driver at the moment. Industry became aware that trade relations/trade partners (e.g. from China or Russia) are not always stable. • E-commerce-dedicated logistics space accounted for an estimated 20 % of total European take-up in 2021 (trend accelerat-ed by Covid-19). An increase in e-commerce and supply chain reconfiguration should continue to boost demand for logistics space over the medium term. In combina-tion with constrained supply, this is forecast to continue to push up prime rents. • Cost of labour high, cost of capital low which leads to the trend of automation. • When you buy something online it takes 3 times more storage place than when you buy it in the retail shop.	**Martin Haller:** Nevertheless, there are still good reasons for off-shoring (costs, capacity, personnel, space, etc.). Not everyone is already paying more for on-shoring.
b	What is your opinion on urban/ last link logistics?	• Last Link thrives on the e-commerce trend. • Parcel service providers are flooding the residential areas. Everyone with the goal of reaching the individual households. Therefore, white label makes no sense from an entrepreneurial point of view. This is still an unresolved problem. (continued on p. 85)	**Thomas Beyerle:** No long-term business model because it is not scalable. Last mile is influ-enced by us consumers. We are the last mile by picking up/bringing a package. It's just around the corner, so I can do it myself. That will be the last mile logistics.

		Similarities	Differences
b	What is your opinion on urban/last link logistics?	(continued) • Urban/last link logistics is a increasing market. The problem is that there is rarely space available and therefore it is hard to find the right assets as an investor. The demand of logistics in a urban setting is currently higher than the supply. A possible solutions are to tear down old park houses in the city, delivery by bike or to develop not efficiently used buildings in the urban area into last mile logistics.	**Bodo Hollung:** Last Mile Logistics: Distribution centre on the outskirts of the city from where parcels are transported to the city centre/distributed directly to the end consumer. Everything was about 1km away from the end consumer, are pick-up stations and no "real" logistics properties. The "real" logistics properties are located either on the outskirts of the city or in the industrial zone (not in the city).
c	What impact have automation and electrification on the logistics sector?	• Electric vehicles reduce environmental pollution and cause less noise. However, they do not solve the area problem. However, due to the low noise level of electric vehicles, delivery times could be extended, i.e. delivered early in the morning until late in the evening. In this way, the trips would be distributed throughout the day and there would be less traffic jams. • Electrification of vehicles is an important change which we already can see today, e.g. Amazon. • Logistics is not dirty – wrong "mindset" • Shift towards greener cities. E.g., in London one pays higher taxes when not using electric cars. Since cities are trying to become greener, it is getting more attractive for them to engange with logistics. • DE has been/is already converted to electric vehicles in order to get to the cities as environmentally friendly as possible. • Logistics properties must accordingly be equipped with charging stations.	–
3	Current Investments		
a	Why is logistics becoming increasingly attractive to investors?	• Logistics is system-relevant. This became visible with Covid (disruption of supply chain). • Logistics real estate has changed more over the years than offices or residential properties. Change/pressure to change means growth. • Investors see potential in urban logistics, rise in e-commere. • Logistis is simply a resilient product, everbody needs it and the population demands online shopping. (continued on p. 86)	**Bodo Hollung:** The asset class was not necessarily pushed by Covid-19. Likewise, nothing remarkable has changed in the supply chains. However, some producers consider having more than just one supplier – avoiding an interruption so that production does not have to be stopped. Covid-19 mainly impacted e-commerce, but otherwise the asset class has always (…)

		Similarities	Differences
a	Why is logistics becoming increasingly attractive to investors?	(continued) • Fulfil the following features: Stable cash flows, low CAPEX, clear asset management capacity, logistics (big box business) is a transparent product that is globally easy to understand & easy to manage → High liquidity (comparison with banknotes → easy to understand globally), good credit rating of tenants, long-term and straightforward contracts → Underwriting, retention rate almost 100 % (how long will the tenant stay after expiry of the "initial" contract?), rental price growth • Advantage of logistics properties: rapid implementation (construction), pipeline can be stopped quickly (e.g. in crises)	(...) been attractive for investors. Demand for logistics real estate remained unchanged before, during and after the coronavirus.
b	How do you assess the current **investment** situation in the European logistics real estate market?	• The attractiveness in logistics can be seen in the declining yields. • Competitive market, loads of player, many transaction. • Cap rates have come down and much bigger volumes are being invested • Prime logistics yields continued to fall in many key European markets in Q4 2021. • Expectations of rental growth, low interest rates and strong investor demand are forecast to push yields lower. • Prices rise or purchasing criteria are eased (currently observed: instead of logistics, light industrial is bought (easier to get) → Dilution of the asset class Logistics	**Ingo Steves:** Net yield compression, logistics yields will overtake office yields. The most "aggressive" yields will be achieved in the logistics real estate sector over the next few years.
4	**ESG**		
a	Where do you see the future of logistics between environmental protection, social aspects, and digital solution?	• ESG is nothing new – topic already existed ten years ago, today only a "new" name (supplemented with Social & Governance) • ESG is becoming a key factor in every asset class. ESG certification are getting more and more important. Eventually everyone is moving into this directions.	–
b	How does the path to sustainable logistics look like?	• Carbon neutral constructions, more wood, recycled materials (less materials), efficient sealing of the surface • Photovoltaic on the roofs, electric vehicles incl. charging station (PV because more power is needed to charge the electric cars), LED lighting, heating with air or ground water heat pumps, geothermal enegery, • Stricter regulations (e.g. high regulations regarding heat protection ordinance in Germany), promotion/incentive programmes • Employee well-being, "reasonable" lounges, "reasonable" company management • AXA in Barcelona: more than 600 electric cars for the last mile distribution • Biodiversity	**Bodo Hollung:** 95 % of the use of a logistics property is the lowest rent: therefore no measures/high construction costs that make the rent more expensive. There is always a drift between sustainable aspects and a low rent.

		Similarities	Differences
c	As an investor, how important is what is happening within the space? Are you providing financing for automation/ improvements?	• LIP: LIP Invest only invests in/on the property. Everything concerning "inner life" is the responsibility of the user/self-financing. In DE, trade tax must be paid as soon as investments arę made in business, therefore only investments in "real" real estate. • SLAM & BEOS: We say that we own the building and the tenants own the machinery. The advantage for us is, that when the machinery of the tenants last e.g. for 25 years and our leasing contract lasts for 10 years, the leasing contract will mostly likely be prolongue. No financing but SLAM includes budget for refurbishment, tenant improvements and ESG into the business plan when acquiring an asset. Invest more Capex to make the building more sustainable, ESG budget (certifications). The technology/building technology that is installed is not a "scope of work" for the investor (not core competency). The investor focuses on the floor, the façade, i.e. the logistics building as such. The building services/software, which refers to the supply chain/operation, is the responsibility of the user/tenant.	**AXA:** • AXA IM has set the following ESG strategy: • Target BREEAM Excellent certification on all new developments • BREEAM Very Good as target for upgrade of existing assets • Refinancing strategy by Green Bonds requiring certification • Innovation for employee retention: WELL Building standard • Reletting strategies focus on Improvement of energy efficiency
5	**Opportunities & Challenges**		
a	What opportunities and challenges will drive the future of logistics real estate? What is the most important driver?	The main driver is the EU taxonomy – the redirection of capital flows to green/sustainable industries. **Challenges:** • Nobody wants logistics on their doorstep. How do I manage to get maximum use of logistics in a conurbation? • There are hardly any jobs created in logistics. • High dynamism, little innovative sector, no money can be set aside, low margins, especially transport logistics (physical movement of goods) • Ukraine war, route through Russia interrupted therefore new supply chains/delivery routes to Asia (lowest development), manufacturing plant in Europe (Eastern Europe due to wage level) • The interest rate development must be taken into account in the returns, EU funds will suffer more than pure DE / CH funds due to their investments e.g. in Poland, the Czech Republic, Slovenia, Hungary (close to Russia) • get new developments, a lot of discipline required → much pressure on the capital now (pressure to deploy money), prime location suffer much less than secondary (continued on p. 88)	–

		Similarities	Differences
a	What opportunities and challenges will drive the future of logistics real estate? What is the most important driver?	(continued) locations, therefore, don't pay the same for secondary locations! (e.g., Winterthur vs. Zurich), making too many compromises on micro-locations and asset characteristics, insufficient differentiation between countries. **Opportunities:** • There's no question that you need logistics. Having the right surfaces and objects is a huge opportunity. • Logistics is basic infrastructure. It is not like a shopping mall or a fancy office building. Therefore, macro-economic risks do not play a major role when it comes to logistics. E-commerce penetration will continue. No concerns on the fundamental drivers. • As a developer/investor you buy a very liquid product, rental price growth, high market potential.	–
b	How will the logistics industry rise to such challenges?	• The logistics industry must become more efficient. This means more efficient route schedules, so that not so many trucks are on the road (no empty runs etc.). • Great potential for optimisation (e.g. returns are no longer allowed). Unfortunately, the focus today is not yet on this. • The logistics industry is innovative in terms of production (technical, IT) but not in the last mile/transport topics – here the industry is naive and sluggish. • The policy must become faster, show fast trade and land use, open mindness vs. Logistics so that excess demand can be met. • Holistic thinking: ESG	**Bodo Hollung:** The logistics industry is one of the most innovative industries that can adapt to change.
6	**Market Outlook**		
a	Which markets would you consider the most attractive in the future for logistics investments and why?	• DE: biggest logistics market in Europe, all trasnport routes go through DE (Hamburg, Nürnberg), lowest volatility • Depending on Ukraine war: Poland, Czech Republic • Netherlands: Rotterdam (the most advanced port in the world, growing strongly), Amsterdam (high ESG standards) • Route: Paris, Marseille, Nyon, Barcelona, Italy with Milan • Direction Istanbul, Austria: Vienna and Lienz become the focus of the war • Finland. Norway, Sweden • UK • CH & Austria: smaller markets • Portugal & Spain (Madrid, Barcelona)	**Bodo Hollung:** UK too risky because of Brexit **Carla Seide:** Tel Aviv because of establishment of start-ups

		Similarities	Differences
7	**Investment Guide**		
a	What will you look at when you develop or acquire an asset and why?	• Location • Purchase price, yields • Indexation/flexibility of the leasing contracts → underwriting rent growth • Geographical diversification → look out for legal enviroment that allow you to increase rent/adapt cash flows • Timing • Efficiency of the asset (in a cargo flow point of view, automation to reduce costs) • ESG • Tenant (profitability operation of the tenant, if the tenant is not profitable, the rents are not being paid), access to staff • Everything connected to the market: demographics, purchase power, growth potential, submarkets, constraints • Infrastructure • Avoid duplication	–
b	Which recommendations are derivable for investors and how can they be implemented in terms of risk/return optimization?	• No investments in stand-alone properties, transport links are important → Develop existing transport corridors through Europe • Diversify the portfolio through the following points: location, type of property, users (trade, production, contact logistics), tenant mix (large, small), lease term, banks/refinancing (only 3–4 properties with a bank). This gives a predictability over 10 years. • Geographical diversification in portfolio, Critical size of portfolio to allow for active asset management, Coordination of global tenant management, No compromise on macro and micro location, No compromise on generic and flexible asset characteristics, Lease structures with reversion potential • We have a lot of fog out there at the moment which makes if difficult to predict a market outlook. The fog is not reflected in the asset prices (they have not come down). Interest rates and inflation high are high. You have to know what you're buying and don't invest like there's always sunshine → Be patient & have a long-term investment strategy/look.	**SLAM:** Add value to existing assets, adding industrial to diversify the risk (SLAM fund EIL) **BEOS Logistics:** Logistics Plattformen, globalagierende Plattformen, Customer Centric Business: von der Grundstücksentwicklung bis zum Asset Management → Komplette Wertschöpfungskette → Als Investor sind wir ständig Ansprechspartner für die Investoren sowie für den Kunden.

Appendix B: Catella Logistics Market Map Europe 2022

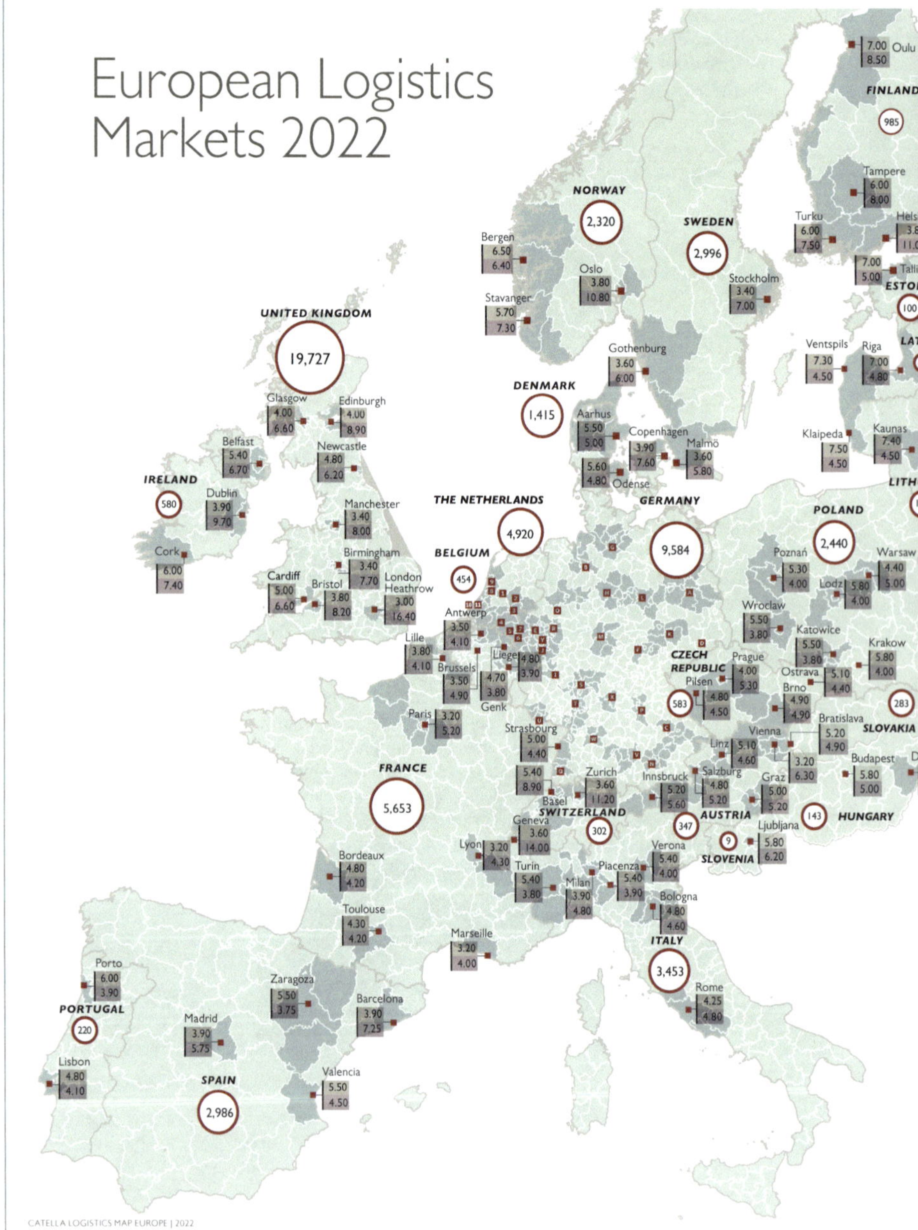

Logistics Properties - risk on the doorstep?

CATELLA

In the second year of the pandemic, the market for logistics proved to be dynamic and crisis-resistant. Rising rental prices and falling prime yields can be observed in almost all European logistics regions. However, the sustained investor interest in the asset class is being met by a changed geopolitical situation in Europe. This leads to a risk assessment, especially in the CEE/SEE countries. We expect a reorganisation of the logistics geography in the next 6 months. It is not without a reason that we included Hungary, Slovenia and Slovakia in our analysis, since the Eastern European markets will become increasingly important. Overall, the logistics sector remains a growth industry.

GERMANY	Prime yield, %	Prime rent €/ sqm/ month
A Berlin	3.00	7.30
B Bremen	3.50	5.00
C Regensburg	3.90	5.80
D Dresden	3.90	5.40
E Duisburg	3.25	5.50
F Erfurt	3.70	4.70
G Hamburg	3.30	6.50
H Hanover	3.50	5.30
I Koblenz	4.20	4.90
J Cologne	3.15	6.00
K Leipzig	3.50	4.90
L Magdeburg	3.60	4.70
M Kassel	4.10	5.20
N Munich	3.10	7.50
O Munster/ Osnabruck	3.50	5.00
P Nuremberg	3.70	6.10
Q Freiburg	4.40	6.00
R Dortmund	4.00	5.30
S Frankfurt	3.40	7.00
T Mannheim/ Heidelberg	3.90	5.60
U Saarbrucken	4.50	4.50
V Augsburg/ Ulm	3.90	6.00
W Stuttgart	3.40	7.10
X Wurzburg	4.70	4.80
Y Dusseldorf	3.05	6.30

THE NETHERLANDS	Prime yield, %	Prime rent €/ sqm/ month
1 Utrecht	3.70	6.10
2 Arnhem	4.00	4.70
3 Nijmegen	4.00	4.70
4 Tilburg	3.50	4.90
5 Eindhoven	3.80	5.20
6 Venlo	3.20	4.90
7 Venray	4.00	4.70
8 Amsterdam Schiphol	3.40	8.00
9 Port of Amsterdam	4.00	5.70
10 Rotterdam - Maasvlakte	4.20	4.50
11 Rotterdam - Distriport	3.70	6.00

>10,000 >5,000 >1,000 >100 <100

Definition of prime yield:
Prime yield equals the yield for a property of the highest quality specification in a prime location within the area. The property should be 100% let at market rent at the time, to blue-chip tenants, with a typical lease term for prime property within that market. The yield should reflect net income received by an investor, expressed as the percentage of the total capital value plus expected acquisition costs.

Definition of prime rent:
Prime rent represents the top open-market rent that can be achieved for a logistics unit (sqm.) per month. The unit itself has to be of the highest quality and be located at the best location of the local market.

4.82 Logistics prime yield net in %

5.82 Logistics prime rent in €/sqm/month

2,593 Logistics transaction volume per country in EUR million, Q1 22

Rent and yield data refers to Q1 22

Description of 112 logistics regions in Europe, based on NUTS3 geographical units for the purpose of creating regions that were as compact as possible.

About Catella
Catella is a leading specialist in property investments and fund management, with operations in 14 countries.
The group has EUR 12 billion in assets under management.
Catella is listed on Nasdaq Stockholm in the Mid Cap segment.

Read more online at catella.com

Research Contacts:
Prof. Dr. Thomas Beyerle
thomas.beyerle@catella.de

Janosh Zalewski
janosh.zalewski@catella.de

Authors

To Tran Quach is a real estate expert and seasoned private banking relationship manager with more than 10 years of banking experience.

As part of her Bachelor of Science in Banking & Finance, she pursued her passion for alternative investments. She specialized in real estate at Zürcher Kantonalbank, where she contributed to the sustainable growth of clients' real estate portfolios through advice and development for land, buildings, and constructions. When she joined Swiss Life Asset Managers, she moved to the investment side, where she now contributes to the success of strategic real estate projects with her enthusiastic personality and strong intercultural communication skills. At the same time, she completed a Master of Science in Real Estate at the University of Lucerne with a focus on logistics real estate.

Prof. Dr. Michael Truebestein FRICS is professor of real estate management and investments as well as Head of the Master of Science in Real Estate (MScRE)-program at Lucerne University (HSLU). Furthermore, he was elected president of the RICS in Switzerland in 2019.

He studied international business administration at the EBS University of Economics and Law (D) and wrote his Ph.D. Thesis at the University of Regensburg (D). He was appointed professor of real estate

T. T. Quach et al., *Logistics Real Estate*, https://doi.org/10.1007/978-3-658-42837-2

management at the University of Kufstein (A) for 5 years (2008–2013). Since 2013 he has been working as a professor of real estate investment and management at Lucerne University/HSLU (CH).

Michael Truebestein is author of various publications in the area of real estate strategies, (international) real estate investments, asset management, real estate markets and digitization. In 2014, he initiated the annual study on "Real Estate Investments and Asset Management" of institutional investors (in cooperation with the ASIP / Swiss Pension Fund Association) and carried out the world's first tokenization of a property in 2019, the "Hello World" in Baar (CH). He serves as a member of the board of directors for an international real estate investment company. In 2021, 2022 and 2023, the Swiss media elected him as one of the 100 most influential and important personalities in the Swiss real estate industry.

Dr. oec. HSG Matthias Daniel Aepli is a lecturer at Lucerne University (HSLU) and an entrepreneur in the real estate sector.

He studied business administration with a major in finance at the university of northwestern Switzerland (FHNW). At the University of St. Gallen (HSG) he completed the Master of Arts program in banking and finance and received his Ph.D. with his thesis in quantitative finance. Matthias Daniel Aepli is author of various publications in the area of real estate management, investment strategies, asset management, corporate financial management and risk management.

Since 2012 Matthias Daniel Aepli has been working as a lecturer of corporate finance, risk management and real estate management at Lucerne University (HSLU) (CH). In addition to his work in academia, he serves as a member of the board of directors and is a renowned serial entrepreneur in the field of real estate.

Made in the USA
Monee, IL
14 September 2026

63193267R00059